OK2 Talk Feelings

Dr Jenny Cozens

KU-678-903

BBC BOOKS

This book accompanies the BBC TV
series OK2. The series was prepared in consultation
with the Continuing Education Programme
Committee and produced
by Richard Foster

Published by BBC Books,
a division of BBC Enterprises Limited,
Woodlands, 80 Wood Lane, London W12 0TT

First published 1991

© Jenny Cozens 1991

ISBN 0 563 36158 1

Set in Trump Mediaeval by Ace Filmsetting Ltd, Frome
Printed and bound in Great Britain by Clays Ltd, St Ives Plc
Cover printed by Clays Ltd, St Ives Plc

Contents

CHAPTER ONE

Saying how you feel

Having feelings is part of being human. If we fail to acknowledge a feeling to ourselves or to others, or if we shut it away so tightly that we're unaware we feel it at all, then we are denying a part of ourselves. This book is about learning to recognise and label the feelings that we have, and finding ways to use them more creatively, so that they become positive initiators of change, rather than something to fear and deny.

The types of feelings we have are determined as much by our physiology as they are by our psychology, or our interpretation of events. For example, if I'm walking through a wood and I receive a blow to the back of my head, my nervous system will instantly be aroused for action: my heart will beat faster, my muscles will tense. I'm designed that way, to protect myself fast against threats. What this arousal makes me feel will depend on my psychology, and what I do about it will depend on how I label my feelings. If I think the blow was from a mugger, I'll feel afraid and probably start to run; if I think it was a small boy playing games, I'll feel angry and will turn to confront him; if I remember that I antagonised someone else yesterday and think this is connected I'll feel guilty or ashamed and I'll act more humbly; if I realise it was just the wind snapping off a branch, I might feel a little tense and I'll probably rid myself of my arousal by rubbing my head harder than it needs, but that's all.

The effects of denial

Since feelings are a combination of our body's normal functioning as well as our psychology, by denying feelings we are inevitably affecting both our psychological functioning and our physical functioning. More and more, scientists are becoming aware of the links between our mind and our body, and realising that shutting off a part of our mind can not only seriously affect the way the whole mind operates, by prompting depression or anxiety for example, but can also cause problems in the way our physical body functions. Once I was chatting to my friend Malcolm about funeral customs and all the differences in various parts of the world, and he began to talk about his father's cremation, and then to remember some of the events surrounding his death. It was clear suddenly that he wanted to cry. He went to the bathroom and came back his usual cheerful self and said he really must get off. A month later I met him in the street. His hands were red and raw. He told me he had the first attack of eczema he'd ever experienced. It started just after he'd seen me last. It was weeping badly.

'It looks like your skin's really grieving,' I said.

'I know. I wonder if we could talk some more,' he answered. When he'd really acknowledged the sadness and guilt he'd felt about losing his father, when he'd said all the things he'd wanted to say to him, the eczema cleared up completely. I realise that this could seem like a good reason never to begin to experience your feelings; but what it really is is an example of how, by denying our natural feelings, we can only live a limited life – there are vast important areas that have to be skirted like minefields – and also that suppression can have damaging physical repercussions. His grief just had to come out somewhere.

The reasons for denial and suppression

We all deny our feelings and repress those we know we have. We do this for a number of reasons. One cause of our denial is that we don't want to feel pain; we seem to think that if we begin to talk about something that once hurt us or that we're frightened or ashamed of, we'll experience all this extra pain and torment. What we forget is that nothing more will be experienced or felt than is already there in our mind and body. Recognising feelings and talking or writing about them doesn't create new pains; it releases old ones. The pain fades as the words leave us.

Researchers are beginning to realise that it is this facing of unwanted thoughts and feelings that creates the change which comes about in psychotherapy. This does not imply that you need psychotherapy to change; most of us can make simple changes to our lives without professional help. But occasionally some may feel they need that extra push and extra help to face what's difficult. Friends are not always able to do this because they also worry about pain: their own and yours. As a friend I did not push Malcolm to talk about his father although I knew that really he should continue; as a therapist I would be prepared to stay with his unhappiness until he had expressed it all.

Some people deny their feelings because they're frightened of hurting other people: 'If I told my father how mad I am at him for what he did to me as a child, I might really let rip. He's an old man now, for heaven's sake.' This is quite true; there's often little point in letting people know how you felt many years ago, but that doesn't stop you expressing those feelings in a letter you don't send, or into a tape-recorder, just to externalise it. Then it can stop eating you away. But also there's every reason to express your newly aroused feelings to others as soon as you can. That way they never get bottled up and so they don't come to feel so dangerous.

✻ *You can test out the idea that unexpressed emotions stay inside you over time by thinking back to some incident from years ago where you were hurt by someone or did something mean yourself or longed to have something someone else had. Try to recall in detail the scene and the feelings you had immediately afterwards. While you're recalling them, notice things that happen to your body: perhaps your throat and chest feel tight as you begin to experience old anger; perhaps your body still involuntarily cringes as you think about old shames. It certainly happens to me, and I know it happens to many of the people I've talked to over the years – so chances are it will be the same for some of you.*

Learning to deny

Of course, one of the main reasons why we don't express our feelings honestly – so that in time they become harder and harder to recognise – is that we are forbidden carefully throughout our childhood to do just that. Babies have the whole gamut of emotions – they rage away, they get shy, feel jealous, are wonderfully self-centred. They express themselves loudly. Of course we don't want to go on behaving like that! But instead of just being taught to behave socially, some children are taught that their feelings are unacceptable or unimportant; that they have no right to be angry, to be sad, to feel jealous. That being selfish or envious is almost sinful. They may be taught to mislabel their feelings: so when they feel angry, they're told they're tired; when they're sad, they're told they're hungry and given a slice of cake; when they're hungry, they're told they can't possibly be.

Little boys and little girls are taught that different emotions are unacceptable: boys can show some of their aggressive feelings but quickly learn they shouldn't cry; girls can show shyness and express themselves occasionally with tears. Little boys grow up into men who equate the declaration of feelings with being female, weak and dependent. 'Emotional' is a characteristic which is still used to distinguish men and women and 'not being like a woman' is how many boys and men define their identity as males. But there's nothing in our nervous systems to cause men to feel any less emotional than women; the feelings men have must go somewhere. For some men, it may be converted to physical disease – like Malcolm's eczema, or heart disease – and the man's repression of his feelings is undoubtedly something to do with why women live longer than men. But both our history and the nine o'clock news also demonstrate the legal and illegal channelling of all this pent-up fear, anger, guilt, shame and envy: we can see it in wars, in football hooliganism, in the House of Commons, in demonstrations, in policemen, in schoolyards and on street corners.

Many women report that they respond to hurt with tears; so when a boss or colleague or subordinate abuses them in some way, instead of being angry they cry. It's true that women do learn to deny their

12

anger just as much as men learn to block their tears, but here's a thought: what if our tears were actually the natural response to hurts which are not life-threatening? What if the tears were there as a vital sign to the other person that hurt had taken place and that he or she should change behaviours? So when the woman manager cries, her male colleague would back off or make his argument more reasonable; if a man cries when his father tells him he's a disappointment to him, the father would respond by wondering why he needs his son to be so great. This argument can apply to world leaders just as well as to the rest of us. Tears may actually be the regulating force for peace in the world that we're all overlooking because men have been forced to learn to respond aggressively to hurt just to distinguish themselves from women. Just a thought!

Whether male or female, many of us still hear the phrases that were used to put the lid on our emotions as children: 'Stop the waterworks'; 'Pull yourself together'; 'Snap out of it'; 'Grow up'. Many children are also taught (because their parents really believe it) that one feeling can negate another: you can't possible love your brother if you also feel jealous of him or hate him for hurting you. It's nonsense. In fact, you can love your brother much, much more if you express occasionally your cross or jealous feelings. This doesn't need to involve hitting him over the head; it might just be a matter of telling him how cross you are. One little girl I know expresses her frustration at having a young brother by fairly regularly drawing a big unflattering picture of him on which she writes: 'I hate Luke today,' and then she tears it up. 'Do you darling?' her mother says. 'He certainly can act beastly sometimes, can't he?' This lets both children know that occasional beastly behaviour doesn't mean the end of love.

✳ *Try this exercise to get an idea of how feelings were dealt with in your house when you were young.*

Sit quietly somewhere and make yourself as comfortable and relaxed as you can. Now start to imagine walking up to the front door of a house you knew as a child. Go in and imagine the rest of your family there. Notice what they're doing, how well you can see them. Begin to remember how you knew your father was cross, and how you knew he was happy. . . . Start to see how your father (or father-figure) showed his cross or angry feelings towards you . . . and how he showed his apprecia- tion of you. . . . Do the same for your mother (or mother-figure). Now think of how you showed your cross feelings, your joy. . . . Notice how you're feeling now, and how your body's acting. Now say goodbye to your family and leave the house and walk away.

Write down as much as you can of your trip. You can try this guided tour of memory with many other emotions – guilt, jealousy, love, suc- cess, for example.

The effects of locking emotions in

What happens if you repress one feeling, like anger, is that all your feelings get repressed. It's like putting your foot on the soft key of a piano: everything – life itself – gets subdued. And it's such hard work. People who come for counselling help will almost always say how tired they are. Of course it's tiring, holding in all that emotion. It takes real energy they would much better enjoy using for some- thing else. Some people use alcohol or drugs to help to deny their feelings, but there is no doubt that, in the long term, this method causes far more problems than it temporarily cures. Not only are the feelings still there to be dealt with in the morning, but the misery and guilt of addiction now needs tackling as well.

Sometimes we cover one feeling with another; for example, we fight when really we want to cry; we eat when really we are feeling guilty; we show angry independence when we would dearly love to say how much we need someone we care about. At other times we transfer our own unacceptable feelings on to someone else. So, before and during the First World War, the British saw all their own aggression as belonging to the Germans, and no doubt the Germans did the same about the Brits. Everyone knows (whether as a parent or a child) how parents sometimes snap at their children because they've been upset by someone else.

A man once asked for help because he worried constantly about harm coming to his new baby. He went through detailed horrors of what some evil man might do to it. When I suggested that he might feel a bit jealous of the baby; that, however much he loved it, maybe

14

life had seemed nicer in some ways before it was born, he began to recognise his own anger and jealousy which he was loading on to some imaginary intruder. Once he'd acknowledged something he had previously been unable to put into words, because it was so 'unacceptable', the worries left him and he was able to enjoy his new offspring and simply be a little sad at the freedom and extra attention that he'd lost.

The emotional continuum

While some people learn to suppress their feelings, because their parents taught them to be restrained just like them, the same lesson can be learnt from parents who are constantly overwhelmed by their feelings – who are so violent or so depressed or so envious, that the child decides he or she cannot possibly ever be angry or sad or envy someone else; it's much too dangerous for everyone, they think. Emotions are, of course, on a continuum: there's blind, murderous rage at one end and a total denial of legitimate irritation at the other; there's awful life-threatening guilt through to a complete lack of any conscience at all; there's constant dreadful fear at one pole and a dangerous disregard for any personal safety at the other.

What we have to learn as we grow up is to be somewhere around the middle of these continuums, and that's the main message of this book. We have to recognise that there is a whole world of difference between actions on the one hand and thoughts and feelings on the other. That acting in anger or in jealousy may have deadly consequences, but having and acknowledging occasional angry or jealous thoughts will never hurt another person. This book is about learning for yourself safe ways to recognise and express what you are feeling, so it doesn't get bottled up and extreme, perhaps to the extent that it ends up being expressed in actions that are damaging. You may also be able to use it to appreciate what someone else is feeling – a partner or child or colleague perhaps – and that will inevitably improve the understanding and honesty of that relationship.

I hope too that the book will provide you with an understanding of where these feelings come from, and help you to explore how much of them belongs to here and how, and how much to the past. This way you may begin to leave behind those things which no longer have relevance for today, and so start to live your life less hampered by old snares and readier for new ways of experiencing your life. Because so may of our present problems do have their roots in childhood, parents may feel they get a poor press in these pages. While many of you will be parents (as I am), all of you have been children, so it's worth realising both for your own understanding and for the sake of your sons and daughters, just how powerful a role – for good and for less good – a parent can play. You may, as I have done myself, feel guilty at times for not acting as a perfect parent. You need to remember that there is no such thing, and that all we can hope and try to be is good enough – as good as we are able.

If you find yourself feeling angry or disturbed at things you read in the book, and deciding it's not for you, read the last chapter before you chuck it aside. In that we look at some of the reasons why you might not want to make things better just yet.

Labelling your feelings

If you repress or deny your feelings, or if you have learnt to be confused about their meaning, you may have trouble understanding just what you are feeling, even if you know it's pretty powerful. Generally you will know that you're feeling uncomfortable and aroused in some way but it's hard to say just what's really going on. When this happens people very often react to the discomfort or tension with anger – they don't want to feel like that so whatever or whoever's doing it must be 'making them' angry. Perhaps they're actually feeling guilty or ashamed or envious, but they have so lost touch with their feelings that all they recognise is the anger. Others don't even recognise that. Because of their childhood experiences, they may have developed the trick of blaming themselves whenever a tinge of anger creeps unconsciously through their undergrowth of emotions. Turning this neatly against themselves may mean their only emotion left is to feel depressed.

So the second aim of the book is to help you, through explanations and other people's experiences, to label your own emotions more accurately. If I recognise that what I'm feeling is actually guilt, I can simply make amends rather than feeling cross with the person who's 'making me' guilty, and then guilty about being cross, and so on, perhaps throughout my life.

For this reason, the best way to tackle this book is to read it right through; that way you will understand more and more fully the boundaries between the different feelings and so learn to distinguish them more usefully. By accurate labelling, by understanding what the cause of that emotion is and whether it belongs to today or maybe to many years ago, and by a variety of methods of sometimes analysing and sometimes expressing that emotion, I know that many of you will have learnt enough to put new understanding into your lives and to begin to let go of cords that tied you to the past. Doing this will let you experience the future more openly and with a greater chance of now knowing those other feelings – of joy, love, confidence and peace.

CHAPTER TWO

Feeling stressed

Men and women have experienced stress since they first climbed down from the trees and began to look upright at the world. If they hadn't decided to face properly what was going on around them they might have avoided some of today's problems, but they wouldn't have travelled so far, from caves and campfires to skyscrapers and central heating! Our evolution has progressed very quickly and part of the speed of it comes from the fact that we see the problems around us and tackle them. Over the centuries, the ordinary stresses and pressures of daily living were the challenges that encouraged us to change, to innovate and to be creative. And they still are.

Right from when we are babies we humans need some challenges in order to learn and develop towards final independence from our parents. Children who are over-protected, hidden from all life's demands and dangers, grow up frightened of the world and unable to consider any ways of changing it to suit themselves. This is an issue not just for individuals, but also for organisations and even societies. The USSR's leaders are currently facing the problem of how to get a nation of people kept dependent for generations, not allowed to try to change their lives themselves, suddenly to come up with bright new ideas for trade and self-sufficiency. We need stresses which challenge us in order to grow.

This is not to say that all stresses are good for you. If we could design an ideal world, it would have pressures which came regularly but not too close together, which were not too large but made demands that stretched you just a little bit more. More importantly, they would contain difficulties which were changeable by you, so that you could feel that you had an effect upon the world. We know that this is often far from the case: stresses frequently come one after the other, or even all at once, giving you little time to recover properly, and many of them are ones that you can have little effect upon. Nevertheless, we need to keep the two sides of stress – the positive and the negative – well in view when we think about what we can do to change. The Chinese word for stress recognises these elements by using two symbols – one for danger and one for opportunity. This illustrates very well that the feeling of stress, once recognised, is a warning, but it is also an opportunity, a signal that it's time to change and to make life better than it is.

Although we hear that stress in everyday life is increasing, it's unlikely that this is really true, and in any case there's no good way ever to find out. But there's no doubt stressers are very different from a hundred, a thousand or ten thousand years ago. Once they concerned running from a marauding bear or fighting the neighbouring tribe; now they may be about worrying whether or not you'll fail an exam, miss a plane, or face an irate and critical boss or parent. The stresses are different, but our physiology hasn't changed at all. It reacts to what we see as threats as it did ten thousand years ago. Then the effects of seeing a pack of wolves rushing towards us would have been that our hearts beat faster pumping blood to our limbs, our gastric system slowed down, our breathing increased, adrenaline released, and so on – all making us able to run fast or fight for our lives. Now, despite living with nothing so obviously dangerous, we still have the same reactions of arousal to things we see as threats but, because the problems are no longer so obvious and can't often be solved by fight or flight in the ways our bodies were designed, we're likely instead to become only too aware of all these physiological sensations.

If you realise that they are simply telling you that something needs to change, then they're an opportunity. If, however, you don't see them as simply a normal reaction of your body to something you see as threatening, then they can become pretty scary in themselves.

One way to understand why we feel stressed and what we can do about it is to see stress as a mismatch between what we see as our capabilities and resources and what we see as the demands and difficulties that are placed upon us (see Figure 1). Of course, our actual capabilities and the actual demands might not be the same as our perceived ones. For example, I might see myself as not having the skills to tackle this new job I just managed to land, and I'm starting really to worry about it: will I make a complete hash of things, will my new boss be dreadfully critical, will I end up being fired and unemployed? And so on. Frightening thoughts! If we look at Figure 1 we can see that my stress comes because I see the demands as greater than the skills to meet them. However, I may be seeing my skills as less than they really are: perhaps I had a parent who never seemed quite satisfied however much I achieved, and now I always see myself as not quite up to the mark. If I gain insight into this I may be able to make my thoughts more positive and realise, for example, that I've always coped well before and there's no reason why I shouldn't do well again, or that, since I was able to land this job, other

Figure 1 – The imbalance that causes stress

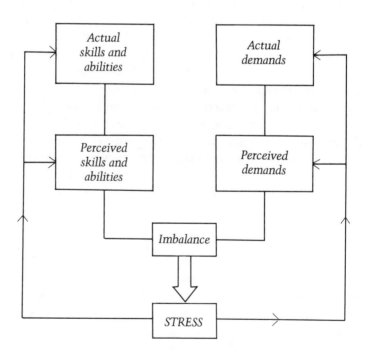

people must think I have the skills and they may know more than me.

Or it might be true that I am short of skills in one area, but I can easily get help or training to make up for that. On the other side, my perception of the demands might be wrong: perhaps I'm inflating them unrealistically? It's never easy to know what's in a job, until you get there, but I could always check things out with my future employer. Finally, it may be that when I begin the job, the demands really are greater than my capabilities and I need to bring in extra help, or organise things differently. As you can see, that gives four places which can cause a mismatch, but also four places where things can be changed.

The eye of the beholder

The other important point to see from the diagram is that stress is always a perception – if I don't *see* the imbalance or the threat then I won't feel stressed! Research suggests that some people see threats more easily than others; sometimes this could be a good thing (for example, if a Rottweiler is tearing down the street towards you it's useful to see it as a threat), but if I find that I see every person in authority as threatening, and other people don't, then I need to concentrate on changing my perceptions rather than continually backing away from situations that cause me to feel stressed.

Some people also experience stress when they have too few demands: for example, those in jobs which are boring and don't stretch them, or people at home with small children who feel that only part of their skills is being used. Even when it's true that our skills do outweigh our capabilities, it's our perceptions of this which make all the difference. I had a friend in the Civil Service who had a very lowly and boring job, but managed to finish his work so fast that he could spend a considerable time writing short stories which eventually were published. Instead of becoming frustrated by his position, he used it to his advantage. Similarly, research in the eighties on men and women who coped well with unemployment showed that these people viewed the whole experience as an opportunity for doing things they'd always wanted to do. Some spent long hours each day developing old yearnings to paint or write; others became politically active, or put enormous energy into a particular charity.

Of course, underload and overload are not always imposed from outside: some people are able to create their own stress, heaping on pressures when perhaps they could get by with far fewer. Shortly after her divorce, April landed a job as a senior secretary in her firm. She really enjoyed the challenge and willingly worked late even when the pressure relaxed a bit. In addition, she applied for a job at night school teaching shorthand and was given two evenings a week. She increased her work for a local charity, and, because she worried about getting little exercise, she took up running each evening. Not surprisingly, she collapsed during a fun run and her doctor suggested she might be under stress.

'Looking back I realise that I was very much filling in every moment after my divorce, perhaps so I didn't have to think about what I'd lost. As well as this, I felt all the time I was in some sort of race, but when I really looked at it I realised the only person I was racing against was myself! I think that I wanted to make up for lost time, the years in my marriage when I felt I hadn't made the most of myself. But what I was doing was far too much for anyone.'

Life events

One form of outside demands or pressures are the everyday hassles and the occasional crises which make up the fabric of our lives. Some of these are controllable, but many are not. These life events may span areas such as a row at work or at home, losing a pet, moving house, having a baby, failing an exam, a parent or a child's illness, separation and divorce, and so on. Considerable research over the years has shown that these life events each have a cost to your health, either physical or psychological: small cheerful events like Christmas have a very small cost, while major events like divorce or death, have a much larger cost. Moving house, job and city at Christmas when a new baby is due and your mother's health is poor would add up to quite a score.

Although we can sometimes space events so that their effects are not so large, they often feel pretty uncontrollable. Because of this it can be more helpful to concentrate instead on looking after yourself. It's surprising how often people forget that they've had a difficult time, and drive themselves just as hard. You need to recognise that, if you have gone through some crisis, you shouldn't expect so much of yourself for a while – give yourself a break.

Recognising the signs of stress

The first step in overcoming stress is to recognise that it's happening to you. For some people this will be very obvious, but others may not realise at all that their back aches more when they are stressed than at other times, or that the sick and dizzy feeling they have each morning is more than the fact that they went to the pub. Irritability is a very common sign of stress but we can sometimes see it as sheer unpleasantness in others or as justified in ourselves. So look at Figure 2. Look down the three lists and see whether you recognise any of them as happening frequently or strongly in yourself. Those

Figure 2 – The symptoms of stress

PHYSICAL	BEHAVIOURS	EMOTIONAL
Heart banging, or racing or missing a beat	More irritable or angry	Worrying
Chest pains	Absence from work	Checking things
Cold sweats	Overwork	Feeling irritable and tense
Dizziness	Avoiding people and situations	Depression
Tingling in fingers and toes	Insomnia	Confidence going down
Headaches	Concentration problems	Agitated
Backaches	Less interest in sex	
Stiff and aching limbs	Drinking and smoking more	
Nausea		
Dry mouth		
Butterflies in your stomach		
Trembling		
Tight breathing		
Muscle tension		
Tiredness		

in the first column will be ones that only you can feel, whereas the other two columns list signs of stress that you can recognise in others as well as in yourself.

Of course, we all show some of these signs at some time or other. As long as they're brief and in response to something obvious like overtaking on the motorway or giving your first speech, then there's no need to think about change. If, however, they come frequently or severely and not always for any apparent reason, first have them checked with your doctor and then, if you're given a shiny bill of health, realise that they might be stress. Michael, a young journalist working nights, took some time to accept that this was the problem:

'I was working extra late on a story and I suddenly realised I was having trouble breathing and my heart was going a bit funny. This got me dead scared, but the scareder I got the worse my breathing was. In the end I just stopped breathing completely. They carted me off to hospital and I remember wondering whether someone else would finish my story and whether I'd still get the by-line! They put various masks over my face and everything came back to normal. The doctor said I'd been hyperventilating, breathing too fast, and asked if I was under a lot of pressure. I denied that I was. I was convinced it was my heart, and it happened twice more before I admitted that maybe it was time to change my life style.'

It always surprises me how often men seem to prefer to have heart disease than admit they're stressed. Women appear to recognise it much more quickly. But things are improving in the 'Real Men Don't Feel Stressed' department: organisations are starting to realise that constant stress affects everyone, even the bosses, and that, if things aren't done to reduce it, then it's bad for the individual and expensive for the organisation itself.

Changing things

Once you're pretty sure it's stress, you need to find out what the cause is and how to change it. Sometimes you'll know exactly why you feel as you do: you'll know you've been doing too many things at once, or you've just discovered that your finances are even worse than you thought, or that your current relationship isn't doing you any good. But sometimes the cause is not so obvious or you don't know enough detail about it. Then you have to become a scientist, observing and recording when you feel better and when you feel worse and, like any good scientist, you can only do this by keeping a detailed account or diary of what happens to you over a day, a week or a month. Buy a notebook and use it regularly. That way you recognise patterns of events.

For example, you may notice that you feel bad in buses, but only when you're on your way to work, never coming home. You might find you have back problems when you're in meetings, but then realise that it's only in meetings where you get cross and don't speak your mind. You may discover you get tension headaches when your mother phones you, but not when your aunty does. You can find that walking home makes you feel much better than sitting in a traffic jam or facing the hassle of public transport. And so on. Diaries like these are wonderful ways to discover things about ourselves we never dared to know!

When you know what's causing your stress, you need to decide whether it can be changed or not. Some factors seem unchangeable but aren't. It's always worth having a go to see if what looks like a brick wall is indeed one or whether it's made of paper after all. For example, you might know that working in an open-plan office makes you have tension headaches, but that's the way things are. Before you decide to change jobs, you could ask your boss if there is any way of making your area quieter or more private so that your work will be more accurate. It just may be that she feels the same way about open-plan as you do, and your request is the stimulus for the change she needs. You won't know if you don't ask.

Similarly, many people say their stress is caused by the world events they view from their armchairs – the starving people, the wars, the terrible environmental threats to our future. Well, these might seem too massive for them to change, but they could make their contribution: they could stop sitting watching television and join an action group. That way they'd feel less helpless.

If, however, you discover that the wall is hard and unyielding, that change in this area at this time is not possible, then stop putting tons of energy into it. As an example, if you find yourself waiting at the bus-stop or in a traffic jam fuming at the lack of buses or movement, realise that you're wasting valuable energy in worrying and cursing, and this is only making you feel worse. The bus will come when it comes. The traffic will move when it moves. There is absolutely nothing you can do about it. You're better relaxing and looking about you so that when you arrive you are that much more able to enjoy whatever you're doing.

Changing yourself

Where you really know that certain things can't be changed, you need to look at what you can do in yourself to make coping with them easier. It might be to do with changing your thoughts. While standing at that bus-stop: 'The bus will come when it comes' can be substituted for, 'Oh no, I'm going to be late again! What will my boss say? When on earth is it coming? Why doesn't the council do something about it?' It might also be to do with changing your actions: getting up earlier because you know the bus is always late, or speaking to your boss to ask if you can work flexi-time instead of having to travel in the rush hour.

In Michael's job as a journalist, there would always be the demands of deadlines: that was an unchangeable part of the job. But he found by keeping a diary that he was actually asking for extra work, taking on more and more because he was anxious to have a good portfolio. He had to tell himself that he could be more successful with a few good stories than a large number of rushed ones. He also realised that he felt much better and achieved more on the odd days that he took himself off for a swim. And then he learnt that he always felt particularly bad if he went to the pub at lunch time. Gradually he changed small things in his life: had some early nights, improved his diet, cut down on his drinking (both alcohol and coffee) and did fewer stories but did them better.

It might be necessary to increase your abilities and resources, and often this means asking for help, something which many of us find difficult but which is sometimes the trigger which sets things changing. We all feel low at times, both men and women, and asking for help is a normal part of ordinary social behaviour. Sometimes elderly people tell me that help isn't worth having if you have to ask for it. Well, that's not my experience. Help is always worth getting, and nowadays people prefer to be asked than to offer, just in case they offend someone!

Stella is a single parent, a mother of two young children. She had some real financial worries, an ex-husband who returned occasionally to beat her up, she was lonely and never went out for fun. She was becoming more and more irritable with the children, and then feeling guilty about it. A chance meeting with an old school friend made her determined to try to change something.

She joined Gingerbread, the group for one-parent families, and, for the first time in ages, felt she wasn't alone with her problems and had the beginnings of a social life again. They encouraged her to go to the local Women's Aid who told her the way to get an injunction to stop her husband's visits. She asked her doctor to refer her to a stop-smoking group and she managed at last to end the habit and so found herself with a little money once again. She bought a book on yoga and learnt how to relax and also felt fitter.

Most important of all, she accepted that things were going to be quite difficult until the girls went to school. Rather than fretting about this and taking it out on them, she decided that this would be their time and the three of them would try to enjoy it as much as they could. The children began behaving better and being less demanding and they all gained much more pleasure from each other. She realised she had far more skills as a mother than she'd ever given herself credit for. She stuck a poster on her bedroom wall. It read: DESPITE GREAT ODDS STELLA HAS ACHIEVED: and there followed a list of all the changes, both big and small, that she managed. She added to it daily.

What she'd done was to seek help to increase her resources, and this led to a decrease in the pressures on her and gave her confidence in finding that she was certainly not alone. She'd increased her skills and her finances and this made the stresses she was unable to change less difficult to bear. She found she wasn't helpless and in fact felt more and more in control of her life as she recognised new areas where she could be effective.

April, the secretary who'd taken on too much, had far more

control over external pressures than Stella. She could make herself a list of her priorities in life and plan them into her week in a more realistic way. She decided that, instead of running, she felt healthier if she broke the day up by having a brisk walk at lunchtime. She programmed in a 'siesta' for herself each day, remembering how much she'd liked it on holiday the year before: each evening, as soon as she got home, she'd lie on the couch for an hour and snooze or sip tea and read. She found her evenings much more productive and yet she was less tired.

These people's strategies illustrate only a few of the infinite number of ways to protect yourself from the negative consequences of stress. Armed with your diary you'll discover (and it's amazing how seldom we know) what makes you feel better and what makes you feel worse. Then it's just a question of increasing the former and decreasing the latter. Here are some other ways that people have found useful.

Ways to change your capabilities and resources

❋ *Get healthy: improve your diet, increase your enjoyable exercise, take some early nights, decrease coffee, alcohol and cigarettes.*

❋ *Learn to relax or meditate: join a yoga class or buy yourself a relaxation tape. Practise it or it won't work!*

❋ *Learn a skill that you enjoy. It may develop a talent or earn you a living or both, but mainly it will increase your confidence.*

❋ *Ask for help – don't wait till it's offered. It might not be.*

Ways to change the demands and pressures on you

❋ *Write down your goals and your priorities and space them out more sensibly. You'll do better if you do fewer.*

❋ *Seek help. Two pairs of hands and two minds are almost always better than one.*

❋ *Join an action group about something you care about which worries you. That way you'll feel less helpless.*

✻ *Don't programme your leisure time: don't think up an impossible list of tasks to do around the home each weekend. You'll either become ill or you'll feel a failure!*

Ways to change your perceptions

✻ *Learn to recognise negative thoughts about your capabilities, and challenge them.*

✻ *Try to understand where the negative thoughts come from: whoever told you you couldn't do it?*

✻ *Write down a list of your successes – remember to count all the 'small' ones too.*

✻ *Ask for feedback now. Don't be afraid, it's never worse than what you're thinking.*

✻ *Ask for guidance on exactly what's expected of you. Is it really as much as you thought?*

✻ *Check that you're not setting yourself too high goals so the demands are always massive and success is unlikely.*

✻ *Break big tasks down into small ones – very small ones – and give yourself a treat each time you finish one. Put the list up on the wall.*

✻ *Accept what can't be changed.*

CHAPTER THREE

Feeling afraid

In the last chapter we talked about stress and how our bodies are reacting normally to real and perceived threats within our environment. When we notice these signs of stress, we can treat them as signals that we should do something differently in our lives to ease the pressures we're under. When people experience anxiety, their physical reactions are very similar to those of stress; they can have any of the symptoms listed in Figure 2 on p. 23. The difference is that in stress, the reaction concerns flight or fight – we are alert to the threat and equipped to take action. We can do something about it. In anxiety, the principal feeling is fear and the principal difference is that we don't any longer feel in control of how we feel nor, to some extent, of how we act. We can't simply have an early night, or take a hot bath or go for a run and the symptoms fade away; in anxiety it feels as if the symptoms have a hold instead on us. Whereas in feeling stressed we are facing something which feels clearly difficult; in anxiety we usually have no idea why we feel so afraid.

In some people the fear that they experience stays constantly, so they're always anxious to some extent, might stay isolated, be very tense a lot of the time, and often feel pretty miserable about their lives – not surprising. Other experiences of fear come about in panic attacks where, out of the blue, often seemingly without cause, people will have a large number of symptoms all at once: their hearts start pounding, they may have cold sweats, feel wobbly at the knees, sometimes sick or in great need of the lavatory. Some wonder if they're going mad; others think they're going to faint or even die. Almost invariably they say they have to leave wherever they are:

those who are inside a room or a building go out; those who are out-side come in. They may go and hide in the toilet or leave the party and sit outside in the dark in their car.

John and Helen were at their friend's birthday party. John knew a lot of the people there and he enjoyed their company and was find-ing it quite fun. He'd had a few drinks, but not many, and he was leaning against a wall watching the interactions and thinking about nothing much. Then he saw what he thought was Helen winking across at a man on the other side of the room.

'My stomach turned over and my heart was crashing round, and I thought I was either going to throw up or die. I really thought this might be a heart attack, but I had this great urge to get out of the room, perhaps because I felt I might make a fool of myself. I shot out the front door and found my car. It was about one in the morning. I sat there trying to get control of my body. Eventually I just felt very trembly and my heart was still racing. I kept taking my pulse. Helen came out about an hour later; she didn't know what had happened to me. She was cross that I'd got upset at her winking – she said it was only a joke – and we had a flaming row. Since then it's happened three or four times. Never as bad as the first, but it usually involved being with other people. Now I've got so I won't go out socially unless I've had quite a bit to drink before I go. I know that's terrible, so basically most of the time I stay home. I don't think Helen realised just how bad it was; I don't suppose anyone does.'

What scares us?

Panic's certainly scary. The word comes from the Greek god Pan who used to jump out at people unexpectedly. John can quite imagine how they might have felt! Other people link their fear to much more recognisable things, and this then becomes a phobia. Although we're all well aware of phobias about spiders, or heights, or enclosed spaces, open spaces, dogs, or aeroplanes, people are sometimes scared stiff of scissors, dolls, unopened letters, thunder, birds, vomit, and almost anything else you can think of. Although all phobias limit people's lives to some extent, some cause no major disruption; for example, a friend of mine who was scared of flying went to extraordinary ends to find cargo ships to take him to the parts of the world he still fancied visiting. Those with claustrophobia, who worry about small spaces, can usually avoid places like lifts, even if it means they might occasionally have to climb up fifteen flights of stairs.

But imagine the discomfort caused by fears about birds – how would you ensure a pigeon or a sparrow never came near you? – or vomit – there's always a chance some child will have had too many hamburgers and ice-cream, and the even more awful chance that you might get a stomach upset yourself. If it's bad, you may never leave your front door. Phobias like this can make life a nightmare: people with thunder phobias spend their lives reading weather forecasts and then don't trust them, while the person who just can't open a letter may do nothing till the bailiffs are banging at the door. Don't laugh at someone with a phobia: they're really no joke.

In agoraphobia people are frightened of open spaces. Some see these as anything outside their house; others find that long corridors, or supermarkets or theatres are what frightens them most. They may find they can travel by car, but not walk, often because they worry about fainting in public; some find they can go out only behind dark glasses. Many are housebound for years. The vast majority of sufferers are women and most of these have very kind husbands who do the shopping and run the errands and make life within their four walls just about manageable.

One of the most common forms of fear is a social phobia, where it's people that scare you most. It may be specific individuals (for example, those in authority or ones who seem to be evaluating you), those of the opposite sex or occasionally of the same sex, or groups of people in general (for example, at parties or in cinemas). Often this fear is to do with feelings of embarrassment and shame (see Chapter 9, p. 103); sometimes it feels linked to worrying about what people will think of you and whether they will criticise you.

Men in particular are often acutely afraid that others are laughing at them. When John, for example, thought hard about the night at the party, he discovered that his fear was partly about the possibility of losing Helen, but also it was in case any other man at the party had seen the wink and was laughing at him. What was happening to him, as for many people with anxiety or panic, was that he was frightened to show his feelings. When he analysed what he'd actually felt at that moment he realised that the fear was covering shame that he'd been humiliated, jealousy that he might have a rival, and anger that he was being made to feel those things. It was the suppression of these feelings that made him panic, not the feelings themselves.

Feeling Sexy

It was Freud we have to thank for pointing out how sex and anxiety are linked in many different ways. Despite a whole century almost passed, we are still to some extent under the shadow of the Victorian era when guilt about sex was at its height and, despite all the apparent liberalisation of the post-war years, there is still great ignorance and fear and shame touching and marring our sexuality.

Honestly, it's all right to feel sexy. It's perfectly natural to feel a flutter for someone other than your partner. It really isn't the end of the world – it's just your physiology working the way it was designed! I'm not suggesting running amok sexually; nor, especially if you are in a relationship, that you should act on your impulses – that often causes more problems in the long run and you can do without them. I'm just saying that if you feel your body warming up towards someone, you don't have to be consumed by guilt or shame, you can instead be pleased your body's working well and perhaps take the feeling to your partner and enjoy yourselves.

Kathleen sought help because she was convinced she had AIDS. She had become terrified of blood and wouldn't even shake hands with anyone who had a sticking plaster on. She worried constantly over the cleanliness of the house, cleaning out the toilets dozens of times a day and washing her hands until they were almost raw. She was consumed with guilt as well that she would pass the illness on to her husband and children. She told how she had been married for two years when she found herself attracted to a man at work. They'd had a bit of a kiss and cuddle behind the filing cabinets, she told her husband about it, he forgave her and that was that. Or it should have been. She kept feeling guilty about what she'd done, and left work as soon as she could to have her first baby. Although there was no way physically that it could be anyone's but her husband's, still she worried about the paternity. Then AIDS loomed up over the horizon and her obsessional thoughts started and wouldn't be turned off. Her husband and her doctor reassured her, but things only got worse. She was wrecking her life, not daring to work anywhere there might be men, unable to enjoy her children, and all because of a kiss years before.

There are other links between sex and anxiety. Many writers have noticed that a large number of women in particular, who have an illness phobia (once called hypochondriacs), have an extremely limited sex life, despite being married. When they come to doctors convinced they have cancer or AIDS and gradually have had every test in the book, however unpleasant, they are often referred to psychologists. Psychologists don't always talk about sex (that's a myth), but it's often a useful question to ask in illness phobias. The length of time since sex stopped within the marriage (if it ever started) can be extraordinary: couples go fifteen or twenty years without acknowledging that something is definitely wrong! They usually haven't talked about it, and it feels as if, rather than admit that the man is for some reason no longer able to get an erection or to have an orgasm, the couple collude in putting their abstinence down to the wife's illness. It would have been so much better for them to seek help together, to learn that erections and orgasms are not always the be-all-and-end-all of sex, rather than to live a lie and learn to worry endlessly about her body instead. Of course people can live healthily and happily without sex, but, if this is the case, make your decision honestly rather than using it to cover up something unhappy and unspoken.

On the other side of the coin, there is a school of thought originating in the Let It All Hang Out Brigade of the Sixties, that if sex doesn't hurt anyone, anything you do is OK. That may be true, but I would urge that you are really honest about whether or not you or your partner is actually being hurt. It's too easy to agree to do things you'd rather not because you don't want to look a fool or a kill-joy, or because you're frightened to end up on your own. Also, if you have been harmed as a child, if you've been physically or sexually abused, then sometimes it's particularly difficult for you to tell what's OK for you and what isn't and you may need some counselling help to let you decide on the limits. For all of us, there will be some personal limit beyond which we feel uneasy or anxious. Only you know what that limit is and whether it's one that's reasonable or that's harming you. It's up to you to speak out and say what's enough.

Fearing getting close

If you've been hurt in a relationship, it's perfectly natural for a while to steer clear of becoming close again. However, if this feeling continues and you are limiting your relationships to such an extent that you're actually lonely or appreciative of how much better life could be, then it may be time to take a risk. For some people this is made more difficult because they may have felt rejected and hurt as a child too and so the present pain is that much harder to bear. Others may fear getting close because they have felt so smothered, overprotected or dominated as a child, and so fear that even a mere acquaintance will begin to take over their lives in that same way.

If this is the case, you need to sort out which fears belong to your childhood and decide to leave them behind. What you couldn't control then is often quite controllable now you are an adult. You can set limits to a relationship, say no, decide just how close you want to be. You need no longer be taken over and crushed by someone else.

Shocks and disasters

The last few years have been filled with a series of disasters which seem unparalleled outside wartime. They have involved thousands of people, either because they were the victims, or their relatives and friends, because they helped either on the scene of the disaster or in the aftermath, or simply because they lived nearby. With so many happening so close together psychologists have been able to record more accurately the symptoms of what they call trauma stress, or post-traumatic stress disorder (PTSD). During the period following, for example, a train crash or a football tragedy, those involved suffer many of the symptoms of anxiety (see Figure 2, p. 23) as well as having nightmares and flashbacks and a great urge to talk about what happened again and again. They report feeling different to those not involved in the tragedy, so find social support sometimes seems less.

The symptoms are a perfectly normal reaction to acute stress and shock and, so long as you look after yourself and talk about what happened very fully to someone who is sympathetic or who was involved, then you will gradually begin to feel better over time. If the event was relatively small – if, for example, you were in an accident, or mugged, or you were a clerk in a building society or bank which was held up and robbed without injury – then you may still feel just as bad for a while as if it had been a major disaster, so don't be tough on yourself and don't think you're being stupid or going mad because it's such a large reaction to such a small raid. Chances are the feelings will go quite quickly if you treat yourself kindly and talk freely about what happened. However, it's very important in all cases of fear that you face what makes you afraid as soon as you can. You might have to force yourself back behind the counter within a day or two, but it's worth the effort in the long run.

A fear of fear

We have seen some of the things which make people afraid, and I expect many of you could add to the list. We know from the chapter on stress that feeling fear is a normal and useful part of the flight or fight reaction to a threat. But in anxiety and panic and phobias, the fear keeps on returning, often for no apparent reason. So John went on having panic attacks, although his wife was no longer winking at strange men, and someone who thinks he remembers his phobia about dogs starting with a large black one that snarled, still feels frightened at next-door's miniature poodle. And in anxiety states, where people feel vaguely (or even badly) anxious all the time, they often can name nothing specific to cause their fear. So what causes this continuing feeling of tension and fear?

Well, the first thing to remember is that you're not going mad. It might feel dreadful, but it isn't a mystery and it isn't an illness – something that's happened to you and which is uncontrollable by you. In fact, what is happening is very much under your control, though it sometimes takes a while to find out how. Basically, you are now suffering from a fear of fear. Those first feelings of apprehension (at best) or panic (at worst) are still with you because the physical changes they bring about – the fast breathing, banging heart, cold sweats, or whatever – are frightening you in themselves. They make you think you're going to have a panic attack or that you're going to die; they make the little dog seem as if it's frightening; they make you convinced you'll be tongue-tied and make a fool of yourself, and so on. You approach the entrance of the supermarket and your heart begins to thump because you remember thinking once that you were going to faint there. As you come closer it thumps harder and you begin to breathe faster and this in turn brings on all the nasty physical sensations that convince you you're going to have a panic attack at least. This awful thought makes you breathe even faster – more symptoms, more awful thoughts, and so on till you're well and truly panicking: a vicious circle if ever there was one. You can see this clearly in the following figure, a simplified version of one first described by Oxford University psychologists Paul Salkovskis and David Clark:

Figure 3 – The cycle that keeps fear going

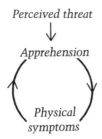

Perceived threat

↓

Apprehension

Physical symptoms

Like many of the emotions discussed in this book, it's not the emotion itself that causes problems, but the vicious circle that may follow. One way or another they happen in most forms of anxiety. For example, if you have a nasty episode with a frightening dog, and then your physical sensations of fear make you see every dog as frightening, you are very unlikely to test out the reality by patting a dog and finding out it's friendly. The cycle is kept going by fear alone. If you were taught as a child that getting angry got you shut up in your room, or seemed to make your mother more depressed, you might still fear anger and so, even without recognising it, a cross thought may turn instantly into the cycle of fear rather than testing out that as an adult you are allowed to be cross sometimes without such unhappy consequences occurring. Similarly, if you feel very shy or afraid of people at any social gathering you may well avoid them as much as you can. If you do go, you are unlikely to contribute much to the conversation in case people come down on you like a ton of bricks or laugh at you or ignore you. So they will think you're not interested in them and include you less and less in their conversation. Your fears will be confirmed and things will feel even worse next time.

The good news is that any circle, vicious or otherwise, can be broken, and often at a number of points. For example, if you take the model of a panic attack, you can see that the circle can be broken at three places: you can learn what the threat is and find ways of no longer seeing it as frightening; you can control the physical signs of fear by learning relaxation and ways to slow down your breathing; and you can learn to change your thoughts from ones which see the physical sensations as an indication of some immediate catastrophe (a panic attack, fainting, or death, for example) to those which see it as simply your body reacting normally and controllably to a threat. That way you stop being afraid of fear itself.

What's the threat?

Although we've talked about a number of things which people say make them afraid, sometimes it's useful to look behind the more obvious threat and see if we can find other underlying anxieties. For example, I've talked about women with agoraphobia being afraid of going outside, and of having nice husbands to help them. Nowadays therapists are increasingly realising that for some of these couples (though by no means all), the problem concerns more a fear on the part of the couple that the woman may find another fellow out in the wide world, rather than any fear of theatres or supermarkets or wide open spaces. The woman is almost kept (and keeps herself) in a gilded cage which protects her from the anxieties of temptation or from feeling strong and confident, and protects her husband from his worries about his own sexual competence as well as jealousies and fears that, if she becomes strong, she might leave him.

I know those of you who are reading this and see yourself as having agoraphobia, or being married to someone who has will be wailing with anger and indignation by now. I can only repeat that the observation doesn't hold true for everybody but it does come from a large body of experience which shows that helping the couple is more useful than helping just the one. So at least think about whether this might hold a grain of truth for you: if it does, you'll change quicker and better by recognising it.

Another example of looking behind the obvious threat is in social phobias. While it's true that our newspapers are fuller of stories of people hurting each other than of dogs, even Rottweilers, causing harm, the fear we have of other people is rarely physical but more commonly to do with feeling you're being evaluated in some way, and fearing that you'll fail the test. Perhaps you can remember childhood situations where you worried about whether you could please your parents enough or whether they would laugh or mock you if you didn't come up to scratch. Perhaps it was a family where making a fool of yourself was regarded as an appalling indignity rather than affectionate fun.

Sometimes too children who grow up with an alcoholic or abusive parent can't get out of the habit of living in dread of something awful happening. This might lead to a general feeling of anxiety, or they may package up all their fears and dump them on one thing only; for example, opening letters might in this way be to do with a fear of the unexpected; a fear of thunder might be to do with early family anger. Alternatively some may develop a series of rituals to try and control their lives: for example, touching objects a certain number of times, checking plugs or locks over and over, going through complicated series of numbers, washing their hands, and so on.

To try to understand what lies behind your feelings, sit down with a blank sheet of paper and a pencil and try to write down the meanings behind the more obvious fear. For example, if you know that social situations make you tremble, try to work out what it is in people that makes you afraid: is it their cruelty, or the feeling you'll be taken advantage of in some way; do you fear that they will smother you or try to make you dependent, or that if you do get close they will then turn round and leave you? Will they find out something about you: that you're 'bad', that you 'always let people down'?

Doing this Kathleen (see p. 33) realised that her feelings over her office cuddle and subsequently over AIDS were not really new. Underneath them was a deep-seated feeling that she was bad, that she was a horrible person. She could quite quickly see the origins of this in the way her parents had looked at her, spoken to her and treated her. Always out enjoying themselves and leaving her alone, they explained this to her by the fact that she was a bad girl and deserved punishing. The AIDS fears were in fact just a modern focus for this awful underlying feeling.

If the words won't come then try drawing your fear instead. Linda, frightened of thunder for as long as she could remember, began drawing the clouds crashing with herself very tiny below them, crouching with her hands tight over her ears. Then she found herself adding faces to the clouds: her mother and father became clearer and clearer, and she realised that what she really feared was anger, and what it meant in her house. There the rows never took place in front of the children, but once they'd been put to bed the thumping and shouting would begin. In the morning everyone would present their usual polite faces at the breakfast table. This was a family who didn't get angry, they told the world.

Understanding these underlying causes will help you to appreciate why you are living in a certain way, why you give yourself the rules and mottoes you do. For example, Linda's rules were to do with never showing anger; John's concerned the feeling that no one would ever stay with him, which he could see was linked to his being adopted, and his adoptive mother dying when he was only eight. The fear that men would laugh at him he put down to his father taunting him about his long hair and laughingly calling him a girl. I wonder if many parents express their angry feelings to their children under the guise of laughter? Others may recognise rules such as 'If I assert myself others will leave me', or 'If I fail at one thing my life will be worthless', or 'I must be in control of everything all the time', or 'If I let myself be sexy I will get out of control and become promiscuous'.

These rules often have the possibility of catastrophe underlying them – I will be a prostitute, my children/partner/parents will desert me, I will end up in skid row, a locked ward. . . . And so on. Understanding where they come from lets you leave them behind, by learning to recognise how they affect your life now, and challenging and changing this.

One way you can do this is to keep a diary of negative thoughts such as that described in Chapter 5 (see pp. 65–6) and learn to challenge them with more rational thoughts. For example, John was able to substitute thoughts such as: 'If Helen winks at someone else, it doesn't mean she'll leave me'; 'If people laugh at me sometimes, my world won't end'. This method is successfully used for treating depression, and is more and more part of the treatment of anxiety and panic.

Another place to tackle all forms of anxiety is to learn a method of relaxation and slow breathing that you can use outside in the real world. Relaxation is a life skill which people often value above all others. It slows your heart rate, lowers your blood pressure and even seems to change your thoughts from resentful and troubled to calm and understanding. You can use it to imagine facing what you fear: attending the meeting, opening the letters, walking to the corner shop, patting the dog next door, whatever. Quite soon you will be able to use it to be in control of the real situation. At the minimum, it gives you fifteen minutes once or twice a day when you are treating yourself to something good and peaceful. If you don't practise it, ask yourself why. Is it because you don't think you deserve it? That it's too simple to help your problem? That you can never do anything properly? These are just more examples of negative thoughts, and need challenging just like any of the others. They are illustrations of the ropes that are binding up your life, but now's the time to realise that the scissors are within your reach.

Facing what you fear

Understanding the underlying causes of anxiety helps in that it allows you to tackle the correct problem rather than the one you or someone close to you has labelled you with. It's very important, but it isn't enough in itself. By far the most important way of tackling the problem is by facing the thing you fear. In the long run the only way over a dog phobia is to pat a dog, the only way to get to enjoy social occasions again is to attend them; if you want to stop compulsively washing your hands, you're going to have to experience not washing them first so that you can recognise that the world really won't cave in, and that you can do it.

Just how dramatic a change facing your fear can bring about was demonstrated to me when I took part in a series of television programmes where people with real problems were counselled for twenty minutes live. The first woman I saw had had panic attacks for thirty years and hadn't left her house without her husband for the past four years. Her husband brought her to the studio and everyone worried that she might dash out in the middle of the programme. Sitting in front of cameras and crew is scary, I can tell you. But she did it. She talked about her problems and listened to what caused panic and she found it a relief that there was a simple explanation. It was, I thought, a beginning at least, provided she follow up all the good advice I'd given her. But actually, she never had another panic attack. Three months later she came to the follow-up programme alone; she was driving again and had got herself a job. For some time I received holiday postcards from around the world. It certainly wasn't twenty minutes of counselling that had made all the difference; I have no doubt that it was publicly doing something so daring and courageous, so that she could never view herself in the same way again, and nor could her friends and relatives.

John faced his present-day fear of desertion by beginning to talk to Helen about their marriage, what she felt about it, how they could both make things better. She welcomed this because she'd known for some time that things were being left unsaid by both of them. He learnt relaxation and began to go again to social events, setting himself one a week, and found that he could enjoy some of them once more. He realised that he was entitled not to enjoy them all, and to select honestly those that gave him pleasure.

In some way you always have to face what you fear, even if it's 'only' a thought like acknowledging that actually you are very angry at how your parent or partner behaved to you. If the threat's an object, like a dog, draw yourself up a hierarchy of feared dogs, and set yourself the task of patting ones that fit the category from the least feared upwards. You don't have to reach the top: I wouldn't dream of patting certain dogs, but that's sense, not a phobia! There will always be a limit for each of us: I wouldn't expect someone scared of flying not to be cured till he or she went gliding; nor someone with a spider phobia to have to stroke a tarantula. So set yourself a reasonable goal for where you want to end up. That way you won't be setting yourself up to fail.

One way that Kathleen faced her fears was to recognise the awful feelings or badness that her parents had given her. She could then begin to find ways to leave this feeling behind her instead of looking for present-day events to explain it. More practically, she was taught relaxation and then confronted with things that scared her now: bloody elastoplasts, shaking hands, using public toilets, touching lavatory seats and not washing her hands until just before she ate. Finally she found she could put her hands in a bowl of blood (provided by the local butcher). Throughout this period her husband and doctor were encouraged not to reassure her, no matter how much she seemed to need it: research has shown that reassurance may briefly bring relief, but the anxiety which follows is even greater. This is because, by reassuring someone, you are stopping them facing their fear. Kathleen learnt to withstand her compulsions with remarkable courage. The feelings that she needed to wash didn't go quickly, but faded gradually with time and as she learnt to look honestly at other aspects of her life.

Things to do about anxiety

❉ *Check out any physical symptoms with your doctor and, if things are OK, recognise that your body is behaving normally in response to threat.*

❉ *Do the exercises at the end of Chapter 2.*

❉ *Keep a diary to learn when you are more anxious, and the thoughts you have then. Challenge these thoughts with more rational ones, and write these down too.*

❋ *Try to recognise, through writing and drawing, the fear that underlies these thoughts, and face it. Talk to a friend about it if it feels too overwhelming.*

❋ *Learn to recognise the cycles that are keeping your anxious feelings going on today, and choose where you will intervene.*

❋ *Learn relaxation and practise it and, while you are relaxed, imagine the thing you fear. Recognise that you can control it with your relaxation.*

❋ *Set yourself a programme to tackle what you fear; for example, to face and speak to a larger number of people every week. Don't set such high goals that you're bound to fail.*

❋ *If reassurance doesn't quickly take away and keep away the fear, then stop people from reassuring you. Chances are it will only be making things worse by stopping you facing what you fear.*

❋ *Give yourself treats and rewards and credit for the courage you're showing.*

❋ *Seek help through your doctor if you feel that the first steps are too difficult. Realise that in doing this you're not an oddity, but one of thousands.*

CHAPTER FOUR

Feeling angry

Anger will pop up right through this book. Anger's like that: it always pops up here and there, often when we don't expect it, sometimes when there seems to be no cause whatsoever. Certainly it's a common symptom of stress, one of the first things people notice about themselves and other people is that when they're stressed they become extra irritable. This is usually just tiredness but, during workshops on stress in the workplace, participants tell me that they seldom become angry in the office or the factory – they don't confront the people who are helping to cause the problem – they wait until they are at home and then load it on the kids or their partners. And then they feel guilty. And then they get angry because guilt is very uncomfortable and we tend to blame the person who makes us guilty. How dare they do that to us? A particularly vicious circle, we've created there!

Anger has popped up right through history. It's involved in events from those described in the Bible (not everybody turned the other cheek, not by any means), through revolutions, terrorist movements, strikes, world wars. History is a catalogue of angry men, often urged on by angry women, taking out their rage on other groups, other races, other nations. When we see this it doubtless confirms our view that anger really is an unacceptable emotion, much better off well buttoned up out of harm's way.

If only it could be that simple. Like the other emotions discussed in this book, anger is a normal physiological response to pain and hurt and injustice, whether actual or threatened. It's what has always let us fight back when we see ourselves attacked, and demand

45

our rights when we feel we have been treated unfairly or unjustly. Because anger is normal, if we see something as hurting us, we will feel some shade of it, from mild irritation through to rage. In this way, if cross feelings are expressed immediately the harm occurs, then it doesn't build it, we don't hold grudges, and society's temper is restored. If I buy you a drink and you don't buy me one, and this continues for some time, my sense of reciprocity – what scientists call moral aggression – would be strongly aroused and I may well end our evening or even our friendship. My irritation, expressed swiftly ('Your round!') when my glass sits empty for a little too long, stops things building up and the relationship ending. In that way the honest expression of resentment protects society by ensuring that mild irritations don't develop into indignant rage.

But this is not what happens nowadays in our civilised, sophisticated societies. Instead we learn, largely through our parents, that the honest expression of negative feelings is unacceptable. Perhaps they sent us to bed whenever we expressed our displeasure, off to our rooms if we sulked or stamped; perhaps they hit us during their own anger or hit each other so that we learnt that anger was not to do with an honest expression of resentment, but with violent actions and rage. Parents fear their children's anger and displeasure. They are never too sure that they are doing things right, even the best of them, and so they quickly become guilty if a child says 'I hate you' or 'You're horrid to me'. Too often they want their child to show only nice acceptable feelings (especially gratitude), not for the child's sake but for their own. Children learn very swiftly, if you want to please parents, you don't show anger; if you love someone, they are taught, you can't possibly hate them too, not even for a moment. So the moments of hate they inevitably feel are replaced by instant guilt which is packaged up and carted off into their future relationships to start all over again.

Anger and illness

Often as adults we fear that if we did become angry we might go completely out of control, we might go mad, we might destroy something or someone we love. But we can't get rid of anger just by trying to ignore it or not recognise it. More and more, scientists are beginning to learn that bottling up strong emotions may be linked to a variety of physical conditions. For example, a group of clinical psychologists in the United States have been considering the links between repressed anger and arthritis. Dr Roger Daldrup from the group told me: 'It's no coincidence that in arthritis our fists are clenched.' Working with chronic pain and arthritic patients, they help them to express their unfinished business – their feelings of hurt, and grief and the anger that attaches to both.

Overall, their research shows benefits in pain reduction after therapy; in some cases, the experience brings about changes that look almost miraculous! I watched a video of one woman, grimacing with pain, weak-voiced and miserable after sixteen years of arthritis, begin gradually to beat the daylights out of a large cushion she'd labelled as her husband (originally described as a wonderful man who helped her do everything). As she begins to catch sight of her resentment, her voice grows louder, changing from a whine to a roar over the session, and her back grows straighter. At the end, laughing and prodding the cushion quite affectionately with her beater, she declares herself pain free. Watching that was the most convincing experience for me of just how powerful anger can be. (As if I didn't know it for myself!)

Its repression has also been linked to the development of cancer. Dr Stephen Greer and associates at King's College Hospital in London have reported certain biochemical characteristics in the immune systems of women who repress their feelings, and have linked these to the possible development and progress of the disease. They consider that a fighting spirit towards the illness gives a better chance of recovery than acceptance does. Certainly there are psychotherapists in the United States, and a few in this country, who are convinced that therapy and the expression of anger is a useful part of treatment, though scientific evidence for this is still weak.

Misdirecting anger

The other important physical disorder linked to anger is heart disease (dis-ease – not feeling comfortable with yourself). Here, the links are not apparently with repressed feelings but with a high level of hostility. Hostile, aggressive, competitive people are much more likely to suffer from coronary problems than others. If this seems like a no-win situation, it isn't: when you're constantly feeling irritable and aggressive towards the world – to colleagues, to people in shops, to the cars around you – chances are this anger belongs to someone specific, either to a partner or to someone in the past such as a parent. In this case just like the others, the true recognition of the feelings is repressed, but with these people, it still bubbles up and over at the least opportunity.

Although it may make those around them feel bad too, there's no doubt that the person it hurts most is the one who's angry, by misdirecting the anger to where it doesn't belong. I once knew a man who would set his alarm for three o'clock every morning so he could play a fugue on his organ and, he hoped, wake the occupant of the next apartment who had once ignored him when he said good morning. Rather than disturb his own sleep for nights on end he would have done much better to look back to his early life and think about a time a parent may perhaps have ignored him. Something must have happened in order to make something so trivial seem so important. In a similar but more seriously self-destructive way, people who have harboured resentment at a restrictive or demanding upbringing may turn it against all authority in ways that may damage themselves, such as dropping out of school or university, making sure they don't use their talent as they could, taking to drugs or dangerous pursuits: generally, cutting off their nose to spite their face.

This misdirection of hostility doesn't just damage our hearts; sometimes it can break them too in the sense that present relationships can be damaged or even ended by anger which belongs somewhere totally different. Steven was suddenly having trouble with his adolescent sons. They were lazy, he said, looked awful, didn't wash enough, wouldn't do their school work but wouldn't get out and get a job either. He lashed out at them frequently, but knew that this wasn't right; apart from hurting their relationship, he also was aware of a terrible rage within himself and was frightened of what might happen if he really let go as his body seemed to want to do. 'What's awful is that it's Jamie, the smaller one, I really want to hit. The other one stands up to me, but Jamie cringes when he sees me coming towards him. It makes me want to hit him really hard.' This upset him and made him feel terribly guilty because it seemed to him he must be less worried about the older one (who was more trouble) because he was scared of his greater strength. 'It's not just that,' he added. 'We went down the RSPCA recently because Jamie wanted a dog, and I found myself wanting to kick the poor little thin ones that looked scared. Jamie wanted one of that kind but I couldn't stand it, so we ended up with nothing.'

After some prompting, he began to talk about his own father, about his coming home after the war and taking over the household 'as if he owned it', hitting Steven's mother and often beating his thirteen-year-old son who was thin and small for his age. He began to see the links between this and his behaviour now towards his sons. He realised that what he wanted to kick and beat and even kill was that little weak side of himself, the one that was hurt and humiliated by his thug of a father. The feelings of hurt and anger had been reawakened by his son's underdeveloped adolescence, but also by the fact that his father was now senile and living in a home. His father's weakness and pathetic existence had also helped to arouse his early feelings once again, especially as now he felt it was too late to confront him with both the hatred he had so often felt, and also with the wasted love he never could get across. Luckily he was a strong and courageous enough person to seek help and to recognise his own deep humiliations and sadness so that his relationship with his own sons could be remedied in time.

Anger and depression

One of the psychological consequences of keeping the lid on anger when we have been hurt is depression, one cause of which is the turning of anger inwards so its barbs hurt only the sufferer and not the one who caused the pain. This is why in depression the person will often see themselves as being to blame for things whether or not they were even involved. For example, a woman may blame herself for being beaten up by her drunken husband, telling herself that, if she were a better wife, he wouldn't need to drink. At the extremes of depression, someone might feel to blame for all the wrongs of the world. We'll talk about this more in the next chapter and in the one on guilt, but it's important to remember that, if you're depressed, what you might be doing is turning anger inwards which should always go outwards.

Sometimes these feelings are turned inwards because we have been made to feel bad and worthless as children. Isobel's main child-hood memory of her father was his poking at her hard with his sharp bony finger. She would be backed into a corner and he would ram his point home about how useless she was, how difficult, how unintelligent, and so on. She still, years later, had frequent night-mares about this, and one day drew a picture of her father's thin hand and stabbing finger, and then she took her scissors and cut the finger off and sliced it into little segments and set fire to it. She was amazed to find the nightmares vanished at once: she had rid herself of that symbol of an unhappy childhood. As a Christian, she was shocked by the strength of her action, but found at last that she was able to forgive her father. I doubt if you can really forgive someone unless you have first honestly acknowledged what you feel about the act done against you.

Isobel had no idea that she was so enraged; she only experienced it as depression. Other people are more aware of their anger and take on a somewhat martyred air rather than make any demands on others. They only experience things in an all-or-nothing way: either they become really wild at people for not doing what they should, or they have to be very submissive and martyrly and do it all them-selves. They recognise that they want things from other people but they never say this, so the conversation and the resentment goes on inside their heads. They need it pointing out that there is a middle route, one where they can be assertive without hitting the roof, can express their resentment or their needs without flying out of con-trol. Chapter 10 (p. 112) on feeling selfish deals with this.

Expressing our resentment

And this middle road is, of course, where we have to be with anger. When psychologists and psychotherapists talk about the need to unbottle your angry feelings, they aren't asking you to go and hit your ageing mother or father over the head with a rolled-up Sunday newspaper, nor with an axe for that matter. The first, and most important thing, is to get in touch with your anger, to recognise that it exists and then to understand just where it comes from. We need to recognise from a young age that, although murder and violence are absolutely wrong, having occasional murderous and violent thoughts is normal. Every child, however rarely, now and then experiences a wish that its parent, or grandparent, or sibling was dead. Of course this is a frightening thought, both because of what it would mean in terms of being left all alone, and because from early on it causes guilt which sweeps the anger neatly into a little untidy pile deep down in the child's mind. The pile gets added to over the years and then the wind comes along – whistled up by some event like Steven's youngest son's reaching adolescence – and the storm begins.

What we need to do, and what we need to teach our children to do, is to express resentments when they happen. It's so much better that a little girl tells her mother she thinks she's mean or horrid when she does, than that she has to smoulder and swallow it down so that a larger and more dangerous resentment builds up gradually, one that is bound to affect the mother–daughter relationship itself, but which will also cause the daughter problems of her own and ones she in turn might pass on to her children. Tom developed tummy aches every morning before school. His parents had started a new business the year before, and it was at a tricky stage and took a lot of their time. Tom needed to go to his gran's each evening for tea, and one or other parent would pick him up from there. His parents were wise enough to realise that the tummy aches were something to do with all this, but couldn't seem to make things better by explaining about the business, as they'd tried to do on several occasions.

In fact, what they needed to do, and found difficult because they were feeling guilty about him, was to let Tom know he could feel mad at them; he didn't have to be polite about what was a situation he resented. It didn't mean they could do anything about it yet – but that also did not imply that Tom had to smile and be understanding. Once they let him say how he felt and how cross he was with them (difficult for him because he knew how anxious they were about the business – they'd told him often enough!), then the aches and pains vanished.

The first step in learning to express our negative feelings is to recognise them for what they are. If you find yourself feeling or being cross with something (often a machine) or someone (often children or other drivers or shop assistants who provide us with apparently good reasons to be mad), check out your feelings properly. Have they happened often lately? Are you under any extra stress? Do you think your amount of irritation or anger is actually justified for what took place (if the answer is no, you don't have to feel guilty; you're just being a detective). If you're not under additional strain and your anger has continued for some time or been out of all proportion to the event, try to work out why it's happening.

Take yourself somewhere quiet where you're alone and relax as much as you can. Is there some particular characteristic of people who make you crosser than others? If there is, see if it reminds you of yourself, either now or at some other time in your life: you might recognise that it's to do with being dependent, or being contemptuous, or rebellious, or weak, or frightened. Was there something from your parents you needed but never got: love, or admiration, or their strength; perhaps being listened to, or being allowed to do well. Spend a little time quietly trying to make these links. Now try again the exercise in Chapter 1 (p. 13): think about the way each parent showed his or her feelings to you and you to them. How were cross feelings shown? How was appreciation and joy shown? Writing about ourselves in this way can also help us to leave old hurts behind.

Present imperfect

But resentments are not all old ones. Think too if there is something in your partner's behaviour towards you that's upsetting you but you won't for some reason express your feelings to him or her? More marriages die through bottled-up anger than for any other feeling, of that I have no doubt. Whether one of you acts the martyr, or refuses to enjoy sex, or goes off and has affairs, or uses drink or sport or work to punish the other, much of the time it's all to do with anger. If this is happening to you, or if you're not talking or you're rowing about little things, ask yourself what you want from your partner that you're just not getting. It might be help, or respect, or affection or sexual pleasure. It might be that you're not allowed an area of independence. Perhaps you think you'd wreck everything if you said how you felt? Or perhaps you think that what you feel is not important. Check out first how much of this actually belongs to your partner and how much belongs to someone earlier – sometimes a previous partner, sometimes a parent.

Jim had grown up with a mother who had schizophrenia and who was, at best, very difficult and at worst very cruel to him, especially as he always appreciated that she was ill and so found it impossible to express his resentment of her behaviour. His first marriage ended after a string of affairs, and now he'd married again and he was clearly very much in love. But he'd already begun seeing someone from his office, staying out late, often coming home drunk. He could watch his wife withdrawing from him, though she never said anything. He knew he felt both love and anger towards her, and he was appalled and confused by his behaviour. He was encouraged to work on the relationship with his mother. He began by speaking into a tape-recorder and telling his mother (who had died some years before) what he missed not having a 'normal' mum. He managed, at first with great difficulty, to tell her how much he resented her cruelty and her absences, and he cried a lot.

He talked to his wife about this and about his behaviour to her and they agreed to try out an exercise which is frequently very useful, especially where expressing your resentment is not one of your strong points. Each of them contracted to say one 'I resent you for' and one 'I appreciate you for' statement to each other every day. It didn't matter how big or how small the reason for their feelings was: it could be 'bringing me a cup of tea', or 'not listening to what I was telling you' or 'showing so much patience when we made love', or 'not enjoying things unless I'm there'. You can work out which one would show resentment, and which one appreciation! It's a very good way to get yourselves back into an honest relationship and one where you can be caring too because it's very hard to be appreciative and loving when you're storing up anger. In fact, the emotions are so linked together that putting the pedal down on anger subdues all the positive feelings as well. The exercise helped them to listen to each other and to attend more and more to real feelings between them, rather than just hearing echoes from the past.

Things to do about anger

❊ *Is your anger being covered up by some other feeling – perhaps by guilt or depression? Try to label carefully what you're actually feeling rather than perhaps burying it under some other blanket. Think about how anger and joy were shown in your family. How is it shown now?*

❊ *If you're feeling generally irritable with life, try to make some links between what's happening to you now and previous wants that were unmet or hurts that went unmentioned.*

❊ *Recognise that feeling resentment and anger, even feeling you could kill someone at times, is quite normal and quite, quite different from being violent, abusive or murderous. Give yourself permission to feel and you're much less likely to act.*

❊ *Practise being open about your feelings to other members of your family and accept their honesty about theirs. You can be sure that no feeling is worse than what's already in our heads.*

❊ *Try the resent/appreciate exercise with your partner or children, even if things are going well. If you worry that it might make things bad when they're good, that's a clue that they're not so good as they could be!*

❊ *Decide to recognise and work off some of your old pains and anger towards your parents or an ex-partner, or some important person in your life. Don't get sidetracked into thinking it's your colleague or boss or teacher – they can be cruel, it's true, but they won't usually affect you in any permanent way.*

❊ *Write a letter or speak into a tape-recorder saying what you wished you'd said earlier. Or focus on an empty chair and imagine the person in that. Try it several times and notice how you feel and what your body's*

doing as you speak or write. Try to use powerful phrases beginning with
'I'; for example, 'I resent you for', 'I hate you for', rather than weak victim phrases, like 'You did this or that to me'. If it's difficult, notice what
it feels like physically to hold it in. If you want to pound the chair, do so,
but make sure you don't hurt yourself: chances are you're pretty good
at that. When you feel finished for the day, say goodbye. That's important. You can always bring them back again whenever you want.

✳ If you can't get in touch with your anger now, then recognise that
maybe you don't want to let that person off the hook just yet.

CHAPTER FIVE

Feeling sad

This chapter covers the constellation of emotions from sadness to depression. In doing this it brings in feeling miserable, feeling lost, feeling gloomy and weary; being desperate, despondent and dejected. It covers having the blues and the mopes and the doldrums, and feeling down. So many sad words, all with the little gradations of difference, give an indication of how common a feeling it really is. They bring to mind a picture of someone with a body sinking down, hands hanging loose and inactive, face and shoulders drooping. Someone withdrawing, lost in their own thoughts, absent to some extent in both body and mind from the social world where the rest of us are busy scurrying around at our daily tasks, finding things important and interesting, planning for our holidays or our retirement, delighting in activities.

Traditionally sadness is seen as a normal healthy reaction to various events, especially those concerning loss. Depression, on the other hand, is seen as rather more abnormal, something to go to the doctor with, something perhaps to take tablets for. Doctors describe the clinical signs of depression as losing appetite and weight and any interest in sex, waking early, often with a sense of foreboding; feeling hopeless about the future, having problems remembering things and making decisions, feeling tired and apathetic. But there is huge variation even within this: some people describe feeling almost nothing at all – a deadening of all emotions – while more rarely some become very agitated and active.

However, many of those working in the field of mental health see depression as very much on a continuum with sadness and part of a normal reaction to life's blows. The loss of activity, the withdrawal, the lack of any sense of the future are, they say, all part of a natural healing process. They are a way of cocooning ourselves from the world at times when we are badly hurt; a period of convalescence for our minds in much the same way that we might convalesce our bodies. The arguments they give for this concern the fact that people do usually become more inactive when they are depressed and do withdraw socially, but also because the vast majority of all sadness and depression goes away eventually even without treatment – what doctors call spontaneous remission.

This is not to say that treatment is unnecessary: it may be very necessary to help you to work through what has happened to you, to make sense of it in relation to other parts of your life, and perhaps to get you to handle life differently in the future. Certainly in cases of depression itself, both antidepressants and psychotherapy can bring about a speedier recovery than leaving people untreated, and the effects of psychotherapy can stop people becoming depressed again in the future. Moreover, people who are very depressed may for a time run a real risk of suicide, and so of course we have to do all we can to help them through what's happening to them.

The emotions from sadness to depression are painful ones, but that doesn't mean that they're abnormal. Sticking your finger in the fire also causes pain, but it too is a normal reaction and a useful one to help teach you about life and behaviour. You might dress the burn to help it to heal more quickly, but you wouldn't anaesthetise the arm in future so that you no longer could feel pain if you touched the flames again. You need to learn to recognise what causes the painful feelings that go beyond sadness, so that you can help to stop them happening again.

Depression and loss

The overriding cause of both sadness and depression is losing something or someone. It might be the loss of a job, or a husband or a girlfriend; it may be that a parent or a friend or a pet dog has died; it could be that you've had a major row with your boss or your daughter or best friend, and fear that you will lose the relationship because of this. Sometimes you have to search more carefully for the loss: perhaps you've had a mastectomy and are sad about losing a part of your body, especially one which helped to form your identity as a woman; perhaps you've lost your hair and long to be the strapping young man you once were; perhaps, recently married or a parent, you've lost your cherished feelings of independence and also some of your individual identity. People become sad and depressed because they see themselves as having lost a battle, or their self-esteem, the good opinion of others. Elderly people are especially prone to loss: obviously their friends are more likely to die, they themselves may have an illness and suffer a loss of mobility and dignity, they may be forced to lose their home and their usual objects and surroundings, and so on.

It isn't always easy to recognise the loss because, especially when we're feeling low, we tend to be much harder on ourselves and so discount our experiences as having no importance. We break our legs, break up with girlfriends or boyfriends, lose our houses and jobs – sometimes all at once – and still wonder why we should be feeling depressed. 'Other people wouldn't be', I'm told. 'I just can't cope with things.' This is one of the reasons that telling a person who's down to pull himself or herself together is such a useless and inappropriate thing to say: you can be sure that people who are miserable are quite convinced that they are useless, hopeless and completely inept compared to the 'friend' who's encouraging them. They feel guilty that they can't just pull themselves together. But they can't. It takes exploration, understanding and time. You are much more useful as a friend if you can help them to look at events, even those they see as terribly small, which might have triggered things off.

The grieving process

In situations where you have lost someone close through death or divorce, then the grieving process is more widely recognised and accepted. Most people know that those who are left will go through a number of stages in coming to terms with the loss, and that these are in some ways necessary. The first and most important stage is to recognise and accept that the loss has taken place – that your spouse or child or parent has gone and will never be returning. In some ways this acceptance is easier, if more painful, when a spouse has died rather than just left. Apart from the fact that there may still be hope of reconciliation in separation and divorce, we are better organised to deal with death: whatever the culture, our funeral services originated with the functions of recognising and demonstrating that death has happened and of dealing with the body in a way that made it clear that the one you loved would never be returning.

Nowadays, our western culture is doing all it can to reduce this exposure to mortality: it's very rare for coffins to be inside the family home, especially opened as they used to be. In crematoriums, the sliding of a coffin in behind a curtain with not even a glimpse of the fire that follows is a very far cry from the funeral pyres of India. It's all too easy to fantasise that your loved one is not really in the coffin at all.

Even with a more traditional funeral, however, it is very common for people to think that they see the person who has died, or feel him or her in the room or even hear them speak. This is a perfectly normal happening in the early days of bereavement, and perhaps a natural way of enabling us to go on saying goodbye more gradually and in our own time. There is no right length of time for any of these stages of grieving to last. However, within a few weeks or months, most people will have accepted the loss enough to clear away the dead person's possessions, to change the room they slept in, and to begin to adjust to life without them.

Carol's husband had died while abroad, and she had not brought his body back for burial. Twelve months later she was still talking about him in the present tense and his room was still lined with his favourite books and music, the wardrobe filled with his clothes and the little mementoes he'd collected over a lifetime. It was only when a friend offered to help her sort through these things and give away all she did not need, that Carol could at last acknowledge his death. Holding a handful of pebbles he'd kept from a holiday twenty years before she began to cry for the first time, and from then she could move on.

The second stage of grieving is to experience the pain and emotion of loss. This is where the sadness really happens, where the tears flow and often the anger too. It's not a time to say 'Don't cry', however hard it is to watch another's pain; nor is it useful to be shocked by the rage that people sometimes express: against the doctor, or relatives, or employers, or even against anyone who is alive when someone loved is dead. Sometimes too they will feel anger at the person who has died for leaving them or for not caring for their health as they should have done. This is of course a difficult emotion to have at a time like this, and you can sometimes help a person who is grieving by saying something like, 'I guess you must feel a bit mad at him sometimes that he wouldn't stop smoking when you asked him.' She or he might not agree at the time, but it will be a relief to them to know that anger is acceptable to you. The more these emotions can flow freely, the sooner people can experience joy again.

The third stage of grief is learning to live without the person, to learn to do the things he or she did for you, to venture out and explore the world on your own again, and to begin to enjoy some aspects of independence. I used to live in the Colne Valley in West Yorkshire. Life there had always been difficult for people and the men, who tended to drink and smoke rather more than most, often died before their wives. The local pub was therefore filled with widows and I couldn't help but notice how jolly they were and what a good time they seemed to have on their halves of mild. When I asked one woman about how she'd coped since losing her husband, she said, 'Well, I loved him, and I was right upset at first. But honest, I've never been so well off in my life.' And she wrote her name up on the pub trip to Torremolinos.

This might not seem a very appropriate story to tell to those of you who are still feeling grief but it does demonstrate that at a certain point you may well feel a little relief as well. It is important not to see this as wicked and certainly not to feel guilty: the fact that you can see yourself becoming independent and enjoying life again, that you can recognise some of the less wonderful aspects of your partner, is absolutely normal and a good thing if you are to move on.

The final task is being able emotionally to leave behind you the person you've lost, so that you can perhaps form another loving relationship. Sometimes people can get stuck here because they see it as a betrayal or because they fear losing someone else and having to go through all that pain again, or perhaps because they really feel quite happy as they are. It's harder to start again after a death than after a divorce and so some people do choose to stay with their memories rather than forming a new partnership. There is absolutely nothing unhealthy about this, or unwise, provided you have passed through the other stages and so long as you are not feeling lonely.

Beginning when you are young

Not everyone's loss is so easy to identify. Matthew felt extremely upset when his boss took early retirement, even though it meant a promotion for him. He had liked and admired his boss, but their relationship was limited to work and he could not understand the intensity of his unhappiness, nor why he should also be feeling guilty. He was encouraged to explore other experiences in his life when he had lost people, and talked about the time when his father left home, when he was only four. He remembered vividly his mother's distress, and his trying all through his childhood to cheer her up and be her little man.

Gradually he began to link his feelings now with the bottled-up feelings he'd had then as a little boy, ones he'd not been able to express then in case he upset his mother. He remembered burying his misery and the anger he felt towards both his parents, but also of feeling guilty because he could only imagine that in some way he was to blame for his father's disappearance. He'd felt guilty too as a child for stepping into his father's shoes, and now this had been particularly awakened by his promotion to his boss's job. Linking this together with the present let him grieve for his father, and dispelled the guilt that had crept into various situations in his life.

We almost always underestimate the effects on children, however young they are, of losing one or other parent whether through divorce or through death or when a brother or sister dies. It isn't so much the event that causes future harm to the child; it's the fact that we often do not let the child express all the feelings they have at the time. Quite often they're not even allowed to feel sad, because their loss is seen as so much less than their surviving parent's. They are very rarely allowed to feel angry at the one who's died, or to explore their guilty feeling about this, or about not being the perfect son or daughter, brother or sister.

The other thing it's hard for us to realise is just how terrified all babies and young children are that their parents will leave them. You can see the anguish on the child's face when the mother unexpectedly leaves the room in a place that they don't know. It's the look that says the child is sure the mother will never return and that he or she will die without her care: really, that's how bad things seem. Gradually the child learns that the mother does return, and it can tolerate longer and longer absences as a result. But that underlying fear never quite leaves us, and is reawakened whenever we experience loss: it's this that makes loss so especially painful again, why often we become almost childlike in our helplessness.

The mid-life crisis

Although our lives are built on the foundation of our childhood, there are certain points in them where different issues arise. As we approach mid-life – and from my experience this seems to be around forty for men and around fifty for women – many of us become aware that the dreams and fantasies we've had since young are never going to come true. This is particularly true for men. They come to realise perhaps that they will never be managing director, or drive the engine, or be a top consultant in a teaching hospital. They see that their wives are not the fantasy women they once hoped for and their children are no longer bundles of joy that could be all the things the father wasn't (rather they are often spotty and adolescent and suddenly doing all the things you never thought they would). The ageing process has begun to show and the baldness is now becoming obvious. Life just isn't what they'd hoped for and they realise now it never will be.

Men approach this crisis in three ways. Some of them take to alcohol in larger and larger doses: this stops them thinking and recognising what's happening to them. It does, of course, also cause havoc to their families and their work, their livers and brains, but for the moment it lets them carry on with those old fantasies. Others find a new younger version of their wife and begin a new family all over again; perhaps they buy a toupee and some snazzy clothes, and pretend the whole process of losing their youth and their dreams just isn't going to happen. We all know how frequently this too is a disaster.

The third way is that many men become sad and often somewhat depressed about this time. It isn't abnormal, even if it seems to come from nowhere; it's a useful and important point in our lives where we can look back at where we've been, appreciate that we are mortal, and leave behind the unrealistic dreams once and for all. By doing this we can begin to enjoy a much fuller and more contented life. This then can be a very productive form of sadness.

Women have far fewer dreams than men, perhaps because the reality of their lives hits them far earlier. The causes of their 'mid-life crises' are somewhat different. Nevertheless, they too are primarily about loss. Many are upset about losing their looks which are more valued in women than in men in our society; their children, who are often leaving home, and their chance to bear more; their parents, who are often around the age that they may die; and quite often their husbands may leave home. When you hear someone putting a woman's depression down to the menopause and her hormones, just remember and note all the other loss events which are happening in her life. If it was all to do with hormones, then women all around the world would become depressed at the menopause. In fact, women's depression in India, for example, goes down at that age, perhaps because they become much more valued and powerful members of society once they are past child-bearing: the very opposite of what happens in western cultures.

Although the role of hormonal change is clearly a factor in some types of post-natal depression, it should again not be allowed to over-ride the social and psychological factors. Women change their status at the birth of their children: they lose their independence, at least to some extent; their finances and freedoms are more limited; career aspirations are often thwarted, and their whole world tends to slow down and be slightly out of line with the rest. The joys of having babies are enormous, but the difficulties often are huge as well, and mothers need to recognise that it's perfectly normal sometimes to resent your baby like mad, and your partner too. This is only bad for you if you bottle it up or turn it against yourself: anger turned inward all too often becomes depression. Of course, I'm not suggesting you take things out on your baby. I'm just saying that sometimes it helps to recognise that you might occasionally resent him or her for your lot. At times like that you should get someone to babysit and take yourself out for a treat, or talk to a friend. People who adopt babies sometimes become depressed too, so look for reasons beyond your hormones so you can do something useful about changing for the better.

Thinking your way to depression

The fear of being abandoned that lies beneath our reaction to loss also lies at the bottom of other types of depression; for example, those associated with guilt and always blaming yourself for everything that goes wrong. As little children, we are pretty sure that if we do things that are bad (like hitting our baby brother on the head or thinking murderous thoughts about our father), or if we fail in things (like learning to put our poo in our potties rather than in our pants or not being as pretty or as bright as our parents seem to want), then our parents will leave us.

These are frequently the roots of depression in people who show obvious negative thinking patterns such as, 'I'm a failure at everything', or 'If I don't get this job, Mary will leave me', or 'This book will never help me. I'm beyond help'. Such thoughts just pop into your head automatically and frequently when you are depressed. Over the last thirty years the links between thoughts like these and depressed mood have been clearly demonstrated, as has the fact that if you can learn to challenge and change these thoughts, your depression is very likely to lift.

The automatic negative thoughts change your mood and your behaviour. You can test this out as soon as you catch yourself thinking one. Say you found yourself thinking 'This book will never help me'. Does the thought make you feel any better? Any happier? Of course it doesn't; chances are it makes you feel worse. Moreover, it will stop you reading on, trying out the exercises, and gaining hope that things could possibly change, even for you.

The best way to recognise these thoughts is to start keeping a diary of them (see Figure 4). Write them down over the period of a week, and see if they form a pattern or group in any way. Often they're about other people not thinking well of you, like 'I'm sure Mary snubbed me. I must have offended her.' Perhaps they involve over-generalisations, like, 'Everything I do is wrong' or 'All people are just out to get you'. They may be unselective, like 'This holiday was just awful', rather than recognising that some bits were good and some were bad. Sometimes they concern thinking you're a failure unless you do everything perfectly: 'These peas aren't salted enough: the whole meal's ruined.' And so on.

Once you've learned to recognise the thoughts, you can add the situation and the time they happened. This is all information for you to check if there's a pattern. Are there more negative thoughts, for example, when you stay up late watching television? Are there fewer when you go for a ride on your bike?

Then you have to learn to challenge and change them. For example, 'I must have offended Mary' might be challenged and changed to: 'She didn't see me' or 'She's clearly not too happy today', et cetera. This will affect your future behaviour as well as not lower-ing your mood as the other one would do. If you think Mary snubbed you, you will snub or avoid her in the future, which will eventually be reciprocated and you will become more isolated. If you see the cause of her behaviour as her unhappiness, you might approach her to talk and actually make the relationship stronger and more supportive. Ask yourself what is the evidence for your previous neg-ative thought, and give yourself a score for how much you really believe it; now do the same as in Figure 4 for the new alternative thoughts. Chances are they'll be at least the same, and usually the more positive thoughts have a much greater probability of being closer to the truth.

You could challenge the other negative thoughts, for example about doing everything wrong, by writing down for a week all the things you do that are right, and remember to put in all the small things too. If you don't succeed at doing this so well, it will be because you're having more negative thoughts about it ('This exer-cise won't work'; 'Mowing the lawn is so trivial, it's not worth put-

Figure 4 – Keeping a diary to record negative thoughts

TIME/ DAY	SITUATION	I FEEL...	%	I THOUGHT...
Saturday 11.30 p.m.	Just been on a date with a new man	Depressed Guilty	75 70	'He didn't enjoy the evening. He thought I was boring. I won't see him again.

I'll never find a partne |
| Monday 10.30 a.m. | My boss walked straight past me without saying hello. | Guilty Angry Miserable | 75 50 70 | 'What have I done wr(He's angry with me ov something.' |

ting that down'), so put those down too and start challenging them! Thinking about the 'awful' holiday and the unsalted peas, you could write too all the good things about the holidays or the meal, however small. Nothing and nobody is all good or all bad: we have to train ourselves to recognise the other side. Often it's a matter of learning to see that your glass is half full, rather than half empty.

Again this pattern of negative thinking comes from our childhood. Perhaps we had parents who implied that we were never good enough, no matter how hard we tried. Or they may have given us the impression that we were only loved for what we could achieve. They might have left us the assumption which we've taken on into our adult love and work relationships that 'Unless I do what other people want, they will reject me'. Again, all these underlying assumptions about ourselves link back to the normal infant's fear of

BELIEF %	INSTEAD I COULD THINK...	BELIEF % NOW	MY FEELINGS NOW WHAT I CAN DO NOW	%
80	I don't know he didn't enjoy it.	55	Depressed	30
			Guilty	25
75	He might always be quiet.	50	I can treat each social event as a learning	
85	He is responsible for the evening as much as me.	60	opportunity. It doesn't have to lead to anything to be O K.	
80	If he doesn't phone again, it isn't the end of the world. It's all good practice in getting back into socialising	25		
75	He's often in a bad	25	Guilty	20
80	mood on Mondays!		Angry	40
	It may be that something at home has gone wrong. I know really it's not to do with me. He doesn't always treat people well – not just me.	20	Miserable I can speak to him as well as he can to me. I can ask him what's wrong rather than worrying about things.	20

being abandoned. It's useful, though by no means always crucial, to try to work back through the rules you have for yourself to discover these assumptions and how they may have come about.

Annabel, for example, had become increasingly upset over the past six months, although she could label no clear event that caused it. She was a part-time social worker, but was thinking about giving it up and becoming a full-time mother. She'd never progressed in career terms as far as people had expected, despite a brilliant beginning as a schoolgirl and initially at Oxford. She described her depression as a great emptiness inside. Her diary came up repeatedly with thoughts about never being any good; wrong to get angry; no one wants someone boring like me for a friend. There were also some clearly envious thoughts about other people's dazzling careers, which then made her feel guilty and ashamed.

Asked to explain what she thought the consequences would be of being no good at things or being boring or becoming angry, she said it would mean that people wouldn't like her. What would that mean to her? That she would be alone. She came to recognise that her relationship with her father and feelings of love from him seemed to be dependent on doing well at school. He showed interest in her only when she shone. Asked what it would mean to her to have a brilliant career, she gradually realised that it would mean she would be betraying her mother in some way. Her mother had no career, and let her daughter know it often. But also Annabel felt that her mother withdrew her affection whenever her daughter did well, or expressed independent thoughts, or became cross at obstacles.

Annabel realised that she was in a cleft stick: be ambitious and you'll please your father but be unloved by your mother; be like your mother and your father will withdraw. Coming to this insight let her appreciate, with great sadness, that she was never loved for herself alone: that neither parent would love her as they should, and that it was time to begin to live her life for herself and her children. She learnt how to recognise and challenge the negative thoughts that continued to come, and became more optimistic, more realistic about her abilities, and more sure that she deserved to do well at what she wanted to do.

Getting cracking

One of the problems of feeling very sad or depressed is that you have no get-up-and-go at all. It makes you slow and tired and the longer it goes on the less you feel like doing anything. If you find yourself just not able to do any of the things that used to make you cheerful, or even to try to attempt the diary exercises I've described above, then you have to get a friend or relative or outside help to give you a little push into action.

There is no doubt at all that activity, especially physical activity, will make you feel better: it physically gets your system moving again and is thought to release biochemicals into your blood stream that actually cheer you up a bit in themselves. Activity will help you to think better and even make you less tired – sleeping and lying around makes someone who's depressed feel more tired than exercise does! Above all it will change the pattern of things, and that is what you want.

Keep a list for a couple of weeks of any activities you do, and what makes you feel better, whether it's because you get actual pleasure from it (like gardening or going to the cinema or having a walk somewhere nice), or because it gives you a sense of achievement (like cleaning the kitchen, or catching a bus to town, or – once again – gardening). You might need to experiment too to try out new things like going to the art gallery or the library, or accepting an invitation to coffee from that old lady at the bus-stop who's always asking you. Cheering her up with your company might even make you feel better. It's important to record how you feel at the time: if you leave it you're quite likely to underestimate the pleasure it gave you. You can also record the times you feel worse – they may be when you're watching television, or lying in bed in the early hours worrying and brooding instead of getting up and having a hot drink and a little read. Now, what you have to do is more and more of what you like, and less and less of what makes you feel worse.

Seeking help and support

If you are depressed, chances are you feel you are the only one like this, and that no one will want to listen to you or help you. You may feel you don't deserve help, or that it won't be much good for you. It's very important not to let these negative thoughts stop you getting support and help if you find you are unable to make progress on your own. Research shows that a lack of social support, of having no one to talk to and confide in, is strongly linked to depression: in other words, not talking to someone will make things worse. When you do, you usually find that the other person understands, because most of us have been very down at times. If it's too difficult to talk to friends, or if things feel desperate, then do go to your doctor and ask for a referral for specialist help. Asking for help is not a sign of weakness; it can be a sign of great strength, and the whole process will begin to give you hope once more that things can be different. And you will find that they can.

Things to do for change

✳ Remember sadness and depression are a normal part of life, and everyone feels them at times. Realise that these are times to reflect and explore and to express some of the feelings that go with them.

✳ If you're grieving for someone or something, give it time. Don't get cross with yourself because you think it's taking too long.

✳ Think of things you may have lost in the past and see if there are links to what is happening to you now.

✳ Seek some support from friends or help from your doctor.

✳ Get yourself moving. Plan in some activities each day even though it really is an effort.

✳ Use a diary to find out what gives you pleasure and what gives you pain and plan into your day more of the former and less of the latter.

✳ Keep a thoughts diary. Write down negative thoughts and how much you believe them, and then write down alternatives and how much you believe these. Learn to do this in your head as well.

✳ Explore by yourself or with help just how these negative thought patterns might have come about.

✳ Recognise when you're angry and why, and find ways to dispel the anger. Bottled-up anger might be turned against yourself and become depression.

✳ If your depression is linked to guilt or shame or envy, read those chapters and find ways to tackle what you feel.

✳ Become your own best friend. Leave old criticisms and betrayals behind and learn to praise yourself and give yourself the rewards and treats that you deserve.

CHAPTER SIX

Feeling guilty

'Each morning when I wake up I feel fine and then I think, "Oh no, this is a day I'm visiting mum," and I feel this tightening behind my eyes and guilt sweeps over me and I'm full of it all day. What's really awful is that I only visit her twice a week in the home she's in, and the guilt comes even stronger on the days I wake up and know I'm not visiting her.'

Sandra, guilt-ridden as she is about her mother, would find it hard to believe that what she's feeling is normal: not the amount or the intensity, but guilt is a perfectly usual and useful emotion which either stops us doing wrong socially or forces us to make amends when we do. It's one of the emotions that is as old as mankind, but it is perhaps more strongly embedded in those in the west than in many other parts of the world. An old Jewish joke goes: A woman knits her son two pairs of socks, a blue pair and a brown pair. When he wears the blue pair the next time he comes to dinner, she asks him: 'So you don't like the brown ones I knitted, eh?' The Christian and Jewish religions in particular are strong on the use of guilt, but also provide ways, through confession or through deprivations at Lent and Yom Kippur, to relieve it.

Psycho-historians consider that guilt is felt and acted upon, not just by individuals, but also by nations as a whole. They see us seeking atonement for something we've done (starting a war, enjoying too much wealth, for example) by electing a harsh and punitive leader who will either make us suffer, or will let us shift our guilt on to another nation and attack it in some way. So they might see the

71

always unwinnable Vietnam war as the means of alleviating the Americans from their guilt at dropping the first and only atomic bombs on another nation. Or the belt-tightening and unemployment of the early Eighties in Britain as a necessary psychological response, brought about by a harsh mother, to the acquisitiveness and affluence of the decades before. With the new and even greater wealth of the late Eighties we are hearing a new word, 'affluentia', to describe the guilty feelings of those in our society who have become suddenly and hugely wealthy, while growing numbers live in poverty. We would expect, if these theories are true, that we might turn to a leader who promised wealth distribution and who chastised the rich. But, as many of us know, there's no reason why you can't be both greedy and guilty.

Guilt is used too in advertising. We are constantly shown images (especially of women, who are more prone to guilt than men) of perfect mothers, wonderful girlfriends, happily coping wives, which are all designed to stretch the gap between what you are and what you could be, with the underlying message that buying this product will help you fill the gap. The images for men all concern their masculinity: they are made to feel not quite masculine unless they drink pints of this, or drive cars like that. The new market for low-alcohol drinks has brought about adverts which at last permit them to stay sober and still be men.

Learning to be guilty

So guilt weaves in and out of our society to such an extent that it feels like an essential part of its fabric. Most philosophers agree that, if we had no guilt at all, it would be a brutal society, one without morals, psychopathic. But, following Freud, they point out that we are not born guilty: this is imposed on us gradually by our parents under the threat of abandonment that we talked about in the last chapter: if I'm not a good child my parents will leave me. Gradually little children learn what pleases and displeases their parents and act more and more according to their rules, until the rules become part of themselves. Most of these rules are fine and let us grow up into loving and caring adults, but often, if we have had a particularly critical parent, we pick up other rules along the way which are much less healthy. What's worse, we will often pick a partner who is also critical and overbearing. It's as if we don't quite trust ourselves to live properly without this.

One way that excess guilt arises is when a child is given mixed messages by one or both its parents. For example, they might be told to be competitive, but always to let others take the biggest slice of cake: this way they'll feel guilty if they don't compete and guilty if they win. Miranda, who runs an advertising agency and has two young children, related at a time she felt stuck in a swamp of guilt, how her father had given her love only for things which he saw as leading to material success, and in this he included her looks. Her mother had been enormously browbeaten by the father, who gave her a very small housekeeping allowance, far too little to buy herself nice clothes. To please her father, dead ten years earlier, she still felt guilty if she didn't work every hour at the office; but thinking about her mother, as she did frequently, she felt guilty about being at the office at all, rather than being constantly with her children. Friends would comment on how she would look dazzlingly fashionable one day and unrecognisably frumpy the next.

Nigel, a young man still living at home, told me: 'My father always tells me to buy the best, and so a lot of what I buy he says is rubbish. But then, if I do buy something really good and expensive, like those stereo headphones, he lets me know I shouldn't be spending so much on myself, that I'm greedy and selfish. I usually end up buying something I don't want just to please him, and then it doesn't seem to please either of us. I really hear him there on my shoulder nagging away while I go round the shop looking!'

Quite often children grow up guilty if, like Sandra, their parents had a very unhappy childhood themselves and told the child about it constantly. This makes children feel responsible in some way for their parents' happiness, and – if a parent is never happy – for his or her unhappiness. Moreover, it means that children in such situations find it very difficult to express any of their own feelings about their childhood. Sandra said: 'Whenever I felt sad or angry at something, if I ever dared to show it, my mum would say "You think you've got it bad; you should have had my childhood, then you might have something to moan about".' It is the denial of the child's feelings that brings about her present guilt.

Wanting to be perfect

Now that Sandra has a family of her own and her mother is in a home nearby, her guilt is caused every morning because she is still denying her genuine feelings. On the days she has to see her mother she feels resentment because she knows the woman will make the visit as unpleasant as she can. But she has never been allowed to feel genuine anger or resentment, so she quickly feels guilty for doing so. On the days she doesn't go to the home, she feels guilty for 'causing' her mother's unhappiness by not being the perfect daughter. She has (because she was given it) some image of what a perfect daughter would be like and how happy that would make her mother. It's only by realising that her mother's unhappiness is her own – nothing to do with Sandra – and that there is no such thing as a perfect mother/ father/daughter/son that she will escape from this guilt. Like all of us, she has to learn to be 'good enough'.

This feeling that you could have been better ('if only I'd done this', or 'if only I'd managed that') is a very common part of grief. Sometimes it feels so unbearable that people try to shift the guilt on to others: this is what sometimes will make a widow, for example, blame another woman for not wearing the right hat to the funeral, or not visiting her husband often enough before he died, or blame his mother for giving him the wrong diet when he was young. In doing this she is expressing her own feelings of inadequacy and guilt. Once she owns them for herself, she can deal with them by realising she did well enough: she may have little regrets at first – we all do that – but she has no need to feel guilt.

Letting go of the fact that we are not totally responsible for a person's happiness or unhappiness can be quite difficult sometimes, because it also means that we have to stop thinking we are all-powerful – in total control of everyone. Patrick was an electrician in a nuclear power station who had, a year before, been promoted to his first managerial post. His job was genuinely very pressured and he could be called out to emergencies day and night. He became depressed, and when he was sent for help he talked about his enormous feelings of responsibility. It turned out that he felt totally responsible for the safety of the plant, which was not true, and a talk with his boss clarified this, but he also felt he was responsible for the personal happiness of his workers, which was completely inappropriate.

This led to a discussion of how he did everything for his wife who was only fifteen when they'd met: he did the shopping and cooking and drove her everywhere. Finally, and not surprisingly, he told how, when he was a child, his mother was always unhappy and how he'd seen it as his job to cheer her up – though, of course, he'd always failed because no child can cure a parent's deep unhappiness and no child should have to try.

It was only when he realised that he didn't have to be responsible for the world, that he could start letting go of his guilt: he could clarify the limits of his work responsibility and begin to let his wife grow up and gain some independence of her own. He had to realise that he was not helping her at all by his previous behaviour. Sandra too had to realise that her mother's unhappiness now was only an extension of what it had always been; that there were men and women in the old people's home who were content and who actually attracted others to them by their smiles and easy-going chats. Others, like her mother, sat there sour and angry and the world stayed well away. She learnt to set limits for seeing her mother and had the courage to make these clear to her, something she confessed she had always fudged before. Knowing clearly that her daughter wouldn't visit that day at least gave her mother the chance of recognising her need for company and an opportunity of trying to socialise more with other people in the home. It wasn't a chance she took, but Sandra began to see that that was her mother's responsibility, not hers.

Sex and greed and rage

From very early on, guilt stops our worst excesses of behaviour – the greed, the sexuality, and the rage of the little infant. This is why most of our guilt as adults hangs somewhere around our dealings with sex and food, and our dealings with anger. Sex and food are linked from the time we take our first sip of milk from the nipple: if the child learns that its hunger and needs are a good and normal part of it, then it will grow up better able to eat normally and to enjoy its sexual appetite. If the mother implies to the infant that its feeding is in some way distasteful, then it will feel rejected and guilty at expressing its needs. This is likely still to be around when adult sexuality begins – so this is the time we see the rise of eating problems like anorexia nervosa (where people starve themselves, and girls stop menstruating and developing breasts) and bulimia (where they stuff themselves and then vomit). Guilt is rarely a part of anorexia, perhaps because the young person's hunger and sexuality are so perfectly controlled, even to the point of death; but it is a dreadful part of bulimia. If either of these eating problems is happening to you, you really must seek professional help – the earlier the better.

In sexuality, adults may find it difficult to enjoy their own sexual yearnings or to let their partners fulfil theirs. If, as children, 'touching themselves' was heavily frowned on or punished, then they may, as adults, be guilty about being touched sexually. The sex manuals that have appeared on the bookstalls over the last twenty years may be full of useful techniques to provide a jollier sex life, but, unless you deal first with any guilt you feel by acknowledging it and handing it back to your parents as their problem, you will still find your sexuality hard to enjoy.

The other reason for problems with sex is that we still have yearnings for the parent of the opposite sex and feel guilty over this. You've probably heard about Oedipus? He was the one who ended up unknowingly sleeping with his mother and murdering his father. Freud took this myth and used it to explain the young boy's yearnings for his mother and the young girl's for her father. Sex is always a part of love, but we often fail to acknowledge that these forbidden fantasies about sex exist, so a boy grows up feeling guilty about childhood (and adult) dreams of his mum and then feels guilty making love to his wife because, in some ways, he's turned her into his mum. And the same happens for daughters.

Geoffrey found that, having married his childhood sweetheart, he had no desire for her at all. In fact, within weeks of marriage, he became impotent with her. He took a mistress and had no problems expressing strong sexual desire with her, explaining to himself that he was doing it because he couldn't fancy his wife. It was not until he could acknowledge that he was treating his wife as a good woman, like his mother, and so one where sex was never thought of, and his lover as a bad woman, a prostitute, that he could begin to heal this split between sexual and non-sexual love and learn to appreciate his wife for being both good and sexy.

In these days when we are beginning to appreciate just how widespread incestuous behaviour really is, we often feel extra guilty as parents if we have a sexual dream about our children. But everybody has them. Dreams and moments of desire hurt no one and are better acknowledged to ourselves than hidden so that they pop up as anxiety, guilt and anger; it's the actual behaviour that is destructive, not the dream.

We have discussed the links between anger and guilt in Chapter 4 (p. 45). As we said there, anger is a perfectly normal reaction to hurt. If these feelings, as well as those strong destructive urges that we experience with jealousy and envy, have been made unacceptable in your early family life, you may have difficulty in dealing with them in yourself and in others when you are an adult. In Miranda's very 'civilised' family, anger was never expressed at all. Her mother got rid of her own anger at the father and envy of her daughter by letting her know all the time what she had lost by giving up her career to have her: she punished Miranda (for the wrongs done to her by her husband) not with anger but with guilt.

Miranda now found any expression of hurt or hatred in her own children quite intolerable: 'I couldn't stand it if I thought they ever felt like that about me', she said when it was suggested that her sons must have hated their parents when they divorced. But she learnt that she could in fact gradually begin to tolerate the open expression of their feelings, and that they could stand hers, including, during a good family talk, the guilt she was feeling over spending so much time at work. They could admit being mad at her sometimes, and this took away their own highly developed guilt at taking any of her precious time for themselves. It didn't necessarily change anyone's behaviour in the short run – she still had to work hard – it just let them have honest feelings about it so they could grow into more independent and healthy adults and would be better able to enjoy relationships with their own partners.

Escaping from guilt – the bad ways

Guilt is such an unpleasant emotion to experience more than occasionally, that we all have various ways to make it feel a little better. Some of these, like Miranda's talk with her sons, are useful and productive; others can cause even greater problems. Many alcoholics and other addicts are using their chosen substance to blot out their guilt, as are gamblers and those with bulimia, and even people addicted to shopping or working. The alcohol, or constant work, or whatever you choose, gives you the high which masks your feelings of guilt, but, when the low inevitably follows, they find the guilt is even greater because now it's mixed with anxieties about what they have done while high: spent too little time with their families, slept around, stolen things, bought something they couldn't afford, gambled away the housekeeping, or eaten an entire cupboard of food, for example. They feel they must take even more of their 'substance' to counter the greater feelings – and so the cycle continues.

Part of the Alcoholics Anonymous (AA) programme is to make people face their guilt in enormous detail, to confess it and then to leave it behind them. Part of the way they do this is to acknowledge every possible guilty act they can remember and then to make amends wherever they can, but the most important part is to acknowledge the guilt rather than keep on hiding it in a fog of alcohol.

Another poor method of dealing with guilt in ourselves is to chuck it at someone else. So a son might say to his mother: 'I'd have got my "A" levels if you hadn't kept on at me to work', ignoring the fact that it was because he did no work that his mother felt she had to keep on at him. There is no way we can really get rid of our guilty feelings unless first we own them for ourselves. While living in Italy as a young woman, I was lent a studio in a large house. There were other studios there, one of which was used by a sculptor of religious statues, whom I'd met briefly at the time I first arrived. One day I was painting away happily when the doors burst open and this huge ferocious man stood ranting at me, telling me of my wickedness at being alone in the building with him, how the whole town would be talking about what we were up to. I was appalled; I'd never even registered that he was there, let alone that he was spending his time in anguish over his 'wicked' thoughts about this young English girl – thoughts he'd dumped on me and the town at large!

Another unsatisfactory way is through masochism, by punishing ourselves cruelly whether physically, sexually or psychologically. For example, some people can only 'enjoy' sex if they're being harmed or hurt in some way, and some couples can only make love after they've had a vicious row – the argument is the punishment for the sex to come. Others punish themselves by taking on the martyr's role, by making sure that nothing they do, or anyone else does for them, is the least bit enjoyable: food, sex, Christmas, holidays, or whatever might bring pleasure. This not only punishes them, but punishes everyone around them too! It's used especially by people who, beneath their guilt, actually feel extremely angry.

A similar method is where you feel you're only entitled to care and attention, or goodies, if you're sick. And so over the years you've had to become sick more and more in order to treat yourself right. A friend of mine who works tremendously hard will only lie down and rest if she's in a bath. That feels legitimate because she's 'doing something' and so doesn't have to listen to that little voice on her shoulder telling her she shouldn't be lazy: cleanliness is, after all, next to godliness, she'd been told. Consequently she spends a considerable time bathing!

Learning to own your guilt

The only way around guilt is to recognise it and then to try to see some of the emotions that it might be covering up, and own them too. One way of doing this is to keep a diary, writing down the thoughts connected with your feelings of guilt and unhappiness in the way explained in Chapter 5 (p. 65). But try too to work back and see where they came from: try writing things down about your parents – your early memories of them. Were they depressed? How did they show love to each other? How did they show their anger?

79

And what happened if you showed yours? Might your mother have been envious of you, and might you have been envious of your mother? How did they react when you became an adolescent? Try honestly to see some of the ways that you might be dealing badly with guilt now: Do you drink more than you should? Do you binge and diet? Do you blame others for things you should accept that you have done wrong? Are you being masochistic or martyrly? Can you give yourself real treats without feeling guilty? Can you rest outside of work time, or do you set yourself another heap of tasks? Are your hours of work much, much too long, and is this really down to you, however much you pretend it's all to do with the job?

Once you've learned more about yourself in this way (and take your time over it), you can begin to challenge some of the thoughts you're having: acknowledging, for example, that you will never be the perfect mother or daughter, father or son, but that you will try to be 'good enough'. You can practise, too, what it feels like to have some of those forbidden feelings: to be angry or jealous or greedy or sexy. Write down how you feel, and again recognise where you're making guilt traps for yourself by capturing and changing thoughts like, 'I shouldn't be jealous of her; she's my mother', or 'I can't be angry with him; he's just a frail old man'. You don't have to behave angry, but you may have every right to feel it. It's giving yourself the right to be honest and to feel again that gradually will take away the excess guilt.

What to do about guilt

❋ *Recognise your guilt and try to understand the emotion that lies behind it. Is it anger, sex, dependency, jealousy?*

❋ *Accept your 'forbidden' wishes and thoughts.*

❋ *Recognise when you project guilty feelings on to others, and decide to stop.*

❋ *Accept that you are responsible for your feelings. Doing this gives you the possibility of changing them and the courage to face things better in the future.*

❋ *Refuse to accept guilt from others.*

❋ *But if you have done wrong, admit it, make amends and leave it behind. That way it won't grow and affect your life and those around you.*

❋ *Stop trying to be perfect: you won't be; nor is anyone else.*

❋ *Learn to feel real concern for yourself and others.*

❋ *Recognise that addictions and eating problems and overwork stem from guilt and decide to do something about it.*

❋ *Learn to give yourself treats. Learn to see you even deserve them!*

CHAPTER SEVEN

Feeling a failure

This chapter could equally have been entitled 'feeling competitive'. These two linked fears – the fear of failing and the fear of succeeding – can stop us playing a full part in the game; can tie us down in cords which ensure that we don't do too well even at those aspects of life for which we have true talent.

Doing it perfectly or not at all

People who are clearly very frightened of failure fall into two groups – those who decide not to try at all or to give themselves a good excuse for failing, and those who do try but feel it has to be done absolutely perfectly, and so are constantly anxious about their performance. The first group includes people who drop out in some way – who never achieve what they could just in case they don't succeed. So you might leave school early under the cover of an adolescent rebellion rather than actually daring to sit your exams and fail them. Or never get close to someone in case the relationship ends. Or never try to make a living through your painting or writing, just in case a gallery or publisher says it doesn't want your stuff. Or you make things so difficult for yourself, that you have a good excuse if you do fail: perhaps you take on far more than you should or agree to move house or sell your car just when you should be making things easier for yourself rather than harder. Or you might get fat or make sure you wreck your beautiful hair so you have a good excuse for not having a relationship.

Other people who fear failure do still strive and make attempts at

82

things although they will be quite anxious about not succeeding. Often they describe themselves as perfectionists. There's nothing wrong with doing things well – that provides us with satisfactions, both large and small, which make life feel good. And if what you are doing is difficult you should feel even better when you succeed. But if you are frightened of failing it's probably because someone else is setting the standards for what will be labelled as success. That may be fine if you're sitting an exam – a healthy fear of failure and desire to pass is what makes you work – but if what you're doing is cleaning the kitchen or teaching a class of eight-year-olds or playing tennis socially, then you need to be able to set yourself some realistic standards to ensure your life is not too worrying and has within it a sense of achievement.

For example, if you are cleaning the kitchen or the car, there are reasonable standards which will ensure your health or the car's paintwork are not at risk. But if your standard is perfection then every scrap of dirt, every tiny chip and stain will cause you misery. Then you are bound always to feel a failure: you've set yourself up that way! Even in jobs like social work and teaching, where there are legal standards set for you, you are likely also to set your own, not too far ahead of these: a social worker can't make the world happy, a teacher can't produce a whole class of bright, achieving and well-behaved children. When you set your standards too high, chances are they are not your own at all, but come from your early experiences. One man I knew had been faced throughout secondary school with his father's disappointed expression when he failed to break records at the high jump; never mind that he frequently won. Needless to say he gradually lost his form and now dislikes sport of any kind, and any challenge makes him worried.

Some people who fear failure worry excessively, others check and recheck their tasks. Mark's mother had grown up with the idea that she, like her mother and grandmother before her, would 'go into service'. She could never quite overcome her astonishment at marrying, not a butler but a doctor, and living in suburbia where he had his practice. Mark couldn't see that she'd got any pleasure from her social elevation; rather, she worried constantly about doing the right thing – always being quite convinced that she wasn't – and about how well Mark was behaving or succeeding at school. It was as if any lack of achievement on his part would be her failure as a mother. Her husband was a cold distant man who also set exacting standards on his wife and his son. There was never any question that Mark would become a doctor too, though it was a constant struggle for him to achieve the necessary grades through school and university. Now a general practitioner in his forties, with both his parents dead, Mark worked longer and longer hours at his surgery. This was partly as a result of his caseload being too large because he found it difficult to refuse new patients, and partly as a result of checking and rechecking everything over and over. He took temperatures and blood pressures three or four times, examined every gland he could feel, whether or not the patient only wanted a day off with a sore throat, and even ran down the street after patients to check their colour again in the daylight.

Of course, it's gratifying for patients to know that they're so well looked after, but even they could accept, which Mark couldn't, that doctors are only human, cannot foresee every eventuality, and are bound to act less than perfectly sometimes. Talking about how bad things had become, Mark could see that taking a calculated risk, as all doctors must do, brought him into a cold sweat that he would lose everything and fail his mother whose life had been so unhappy, and his father who still seemed to 'sit on my back and watch my every move'. Because his father was so remote and unknown, he had fantasised that he was a perfect doctor who never made a mistake, never missed a thing, and it was these impossible standards that he then set himself.

Most people who check things a lot, or clean obsessively are fearing something which they find hard to name – the mess, the uncontrollable chaos, the pit, total shame are some of the descriptions I've heard. If you find yourself doing this, take some time to work out what you fear: what would it mean if the kitchen was dirty? Would it mean your family might get sick? Your neighbours wouldn't talk to you? What would that mean? And so on. You will often come back to the underlying fear of being abandoned by everyone, the fear that underlies so many others – or of some black hole, uncontrollable mess, that you can't quite put words to. Chances are you can't put words to it because what you fear might have happened before you had words – it might have been the disgusted look on your mother's face as she undid another dirty nappy or ripped off your damp or messy sheets. It doesn't matter that you can't remember that, what matters is that you realise that the mess and the fear of abandonment belonged all that time ago – it doesn't belong to now, today.

Today you can risk lowering your standards gradually to see what happens. Set yourself a diminishing number of times to clean or to check: today I will only clean the toilet twice, only wash my hands before I eat, only check each patient's temperature if I can feel that they are hot. Today I'll start trusting myself.

Sexual relations certainly suffer from a fear of failure. If you're anxious about doing it just like the movies, then you're bound to enjoy it less. Someone has written on a bridge on the road to York 'SEX IS FUNNY', and each time I pass it cheers me up. Sex is funny and it should be fun. There is no perfect way to do it, no one rule-bound manner to make it good. It's as much about comfort and cuddles as about panting and orgasms. So, if you're in a sexual relationship, give yourselves permission simply to enjoy the experience rather than acting as though you're sitting an examination with only one acceptable outcome.

Letting go of the rule-book

The other thing to do is to learn to recognise the thoughts that tie you up in a fear of failure. If you do a piece of work, and you feel like going on and on in case it isn't good enough, write down what you're thinking (see Figure 4, p. 66, for how to do this in more detail). It might be 'This just isn't good enough; I know my boss won't like it'. Give yourself a percentage score for how much you believe that (let's say 85%) and how you feel when you think these thoughts ('worried and miserable' perhaps). Now write down some rational responses. They might be: 'I'm regarded as OK at my job, so why should it be wrong; my boss has never said I'm working badly; I can easily ask for feedback on this piece of work at this stage; if he/she says I need to do more, then that's O K: nothing he/she can say will be worse than I'm thinking they'll say, and if it was the same I'd be no worse off.' Now check how much you believe each new thought (perhaps 90%), and how you feel after thinking them ('relieved, hopeful'?). I'd be very surprised if it wasn't considerably better, but don't expect perfect scores (you perfectionists sometimes do!) – as long as it's a bit better, things are changing.

Feeling you might fail

If you have a strong fear of failure, then chances are you will antici-pate not managing to change at all. You will be thinking of all the reasons you will fail, and what that will feel like, rather than think-ing that even one small positive step will be better than things are now. If you catch yourself deciding not to change for this reason, try the following arguments.

❋ *I only have to have a go at some of the exercises; not produce a per-fect performance.*

❋ *I can learn more about my thoughts and feelings by trying to do something new than by wrapping myself in a prison of cotton-wool.*

❋ *Do I feel good not doing it!*

❋ *If I wait till I'm feeling better before I do anything, I'll never do any-thing.*

❋ *I don't need to expect a miracle, just a step in the right direction.*

Sometimes you might decide not to go for help because you might fail at the relationship with the counsellor or therapist. This is not so strange as it sounds: if you have been made to feel that you fail people you're quite likely to think that you should achieve some-thing in therapy, not for yourself, but for the therapist. This is never true. Any good therapist will be happy that you feel OK again, but only for your benefit, not for his or hers. They are there to help you – not the other way round – and if you find this uncomfortable or if you feel you're not the 'perfect' client, let them know about it. That way it's out in the open and can be discussed.

Do the same exercise if you are honest enough to admit that you're not even beginning to tackle things just in case you fail. Again, ask whom you think you're failing, and recognise that the only person who's suffering now is you. Decide you'll be a scientist and study yourself having a go at things you'd rather avoid. If you're frightened of relationships ask ten girls (or boys) to dance at the disco, and write about how you felt when they accepted or refused. If you're lonely, try talking to someone each day at the bus-stop, in a shop. They may be lonely too. Challenge yourself: are you making sure you don't recognise acceptance when it happens, or that you won't see it as any sort of success? Did you stand on their feet when you asked them, just to make sure they looked pained? Set yourself even more daring tasks next week. You have nothing to lose. If you feel you have, then spend some time working out what it is.

Making sure you don't succeed

Some people go the other way. While the natural human drive is towards aspiring, and enjoying pushing yourself forward, some people fear competition and success and may go to great ends to sabotage themselves. Patricia was brought up as a bit of a hot-house child. Her mother taught her to read by the age of three and she was two years ahead of everyone at school. The pressure to succeed at everything was immense. This made friendships difficult, especially in high school when her child's small frame seemed constantly surrounded by massive menacing adolescent girls with breasts and boyfriends. Despite the two-year age gap, she usually came second in the class, much to her parents' disappointment, and got to university with straight A's. Just before her finals she went on a bender. She stayed out each night dancing, drinking, and trying her first soft drugs. She still managed to get an upper second, but the first-class degree that her parents longed for was gone for ever.

This was a pattern based on anger (see Chapter 4, p. 45) which was to go on throughout her career and even her relationships. So she 'spoilt' her first marriage by bouts of drinking and unpleasant behaviour at times which caused maximum embarrassment to her husband. What she was doing was expressing her anger and resentment at her parents' demands, taking these feelings into the present day whenever anyone showed they expected something of her. Such a way of living your life might come from a very demanding background, like hers, or from one which is restrictive in a way which produces an adolescent reaction – 'if you tell me I must/mustn't do it, then I won't/will' – but one which lasts through life in a very self-destructive way.

Sometimes the self-destruction comes through guilt. George, an accountant, always sailed 'close to the wind'. Although his business was successful he would often take on risky deals edging on the illegal. He didn't need the money – he'd made more than he knew what to do with – but he still took the risks. Eventually he was imprisoned for fraud. While he was inside he negotiated a business deal with a man who was clearly more crooked than a country lane, signing over the value of his hugely expensive house in order to finance it. Needless to say, the man and his booty vanished, George and his wife lost their house, and had to start from nothing all over again, with no career left to help. When he was persuaded that this was all more than bad luck or momentary poor judgment, he began to look honestly at his life. Similar to Annabel in Chapter 5 (p. 67), he realised that he always felt guilty about any success because he felt it meant 'doing down my dad' who had never done too well at anything. He felt the urge to compete against his father, and to win, and then to strip himself of his winnings. Once he realised both the strength of his competition and of his self-destruction, then he could stop, but what a hard route he'd taken up till then!

Sometimes this problem with competition and success comes about because you've been told at some level that you have no right to succeed – you don't deserve to do well because you're bad. Parents can get this across to children in all sorts of subtle ways, even while urging them on. Often they do it because they're envious, sometimes because they're locked into an anger of their own that they're taking out on their children. Where a parent has died or gone away, especially one of the same sex, children may create these feelings for themselves: they may imagine that some angry thought made the parent die or leave, or that they went because the child was so bad. They too will often find it hard to succeed. So Paul dropped out of law school when his father, with whom he'd fought right through adolescence, died suddenly. He began writing but stopped once his first book was published. He destroyed two marriages. And all because he felt he didn't deserve to do well, to be happy; perhaps he didn't even feel he deserved to be alive now his father was dead. Giving children a full chance to grieve their loss (something particularly difficult to do in a divorce where you might only want them to share your anger at the one who left) and to express their worries about their role in it, will usually be enough to stop this fear developing.

Two rods to beat yourself with

Some people are stuck between both the fear of failing and the fear of succeeding. Geoff was from the other side of town, from the dark rows of back-to-backs which tucked themselves in between the steel works. He crossed the city to go to a grammar school in the leafy suburbs. His father and elder brother, as well as the local boys, goaded him and mocked him for being 'a cut above', for being snooty (although they gave him no chance to be anything else). He became very anxious while he was doing his 'A' levels, and ended up going to college and studying electronics at which he had an exceptional talent. In the family firm he joined he was treated well, because he was so good, but also excluded, because he wasn't part of the family (a situation he remembered from his childhood). He had an opportunity to start his own company with an invention he'd developed, but didn't dare to go ahead and found himself becoming anxious once again.

He was taught relaxation, and began to put it into practice at times he felt anxious. More important, he used it to think about his fear – when it came and what he was afraid of. He kept a diary of negative thoughts to help him do this, and found there were both thoughts to do with a fear of failing, which he traced back to a certainty that a single failure would mean he was back in those back streets among people who would for ever torment him, and a fear of succeeding which he realised he felt would stop his father ever loving him, ever being pleased with him. He was stuck firm between them both, as he'd been before when he faced failing or succeeding at his 'A' levels.

He taught himself to challenge these thoughts with more rational ones, such as: 'I don't have to succeed at everything I do' and 'One failure won't bring about permanent catastrophe', and even 'I survived that environment as a child; I can certainly do it as a man'. To help in this, he went through the Worst Scenario routine: what is the worst thing that could happen to you if you started your own business. He and his wife went over every awful outcome they could think of, and wrote down the strategies they'd use to cope with each. He realised that his fear had been stopping him plan anything properly, and he was actually much better at the business side than he'd let himself think. Bringing his wife in on his anxieties and conflicts was enormously useful. He was able to reassure himself that, rather than being on the brink of walking out as he'd imagined, she was right with him in their venture and even that she would actually enjoy being part of the challenge.

He realised, with great sadness and a lot of tears, that actually his father would never love him as he should, that he would always prefer his elder son, and that making sure he didn't succeed would never win him round. In this way he could finally leave the confines of his conflict, and decide to take a risk for himself and to succeed for himself.

Things to do about feeling a failure

✱ Consider what your standards really are. Where do they come from? Are they realistic? Check with friends and colleagues about their standards. Recognise the huge variety.

✱ Don't hide behind the curtain of 'perfectionist' – it's usually a shorthand word for worried and uncomfortable.

✱ Realise that life is risky: there are no certainties. You will never be able to control every eventuality. You don't even have to try!

✱ Recognise that everyone fails sometimes: their world doesn't end; they don't have to end up penniless or friendless because of it.

✱ Keep a diary to try to work out why failing is so frightening for you. Is there a parent whispering in your ear about what will happen if you don't succeed! Decide you'll leave that voice behind by learning to write down rational responses to negative thoughts.

✳ Work out the Worst Scenario and how you'd cope – not perfectly, but well enough.

✳ Practise 'failing'! Don't clean the house so perfectly; don't try to cook the perfect meal; decide against film-star sex; don't recheck the work you've done. What are the results? Is it a real catastrophe? Can you cope with it? Remember your coping doesn't have to be perfect, not by any means.

✳ Make yourself take 'risks' by trying things you'd rather avoid – either in case you might fail, or in case you might succeed! Be a scientist and record your activities and reactions.

✳ If you're frightened of success or winning or looking good, think about who it seems will suffer or be worse off because of it. Check whether you think you deserve things. Ask yourself where those feelings come from.

✳ Are you not doing things just because someone has said you should, or doing things just because they said you mustn't? What's the result of this for you? Can you see a pattern of it in your life? Where did it start?

✳ Check that you're not putting obstacles in your way to make success less likely/more difficult, to provide you with a really good excuse for failing!

CHAPTER EIGHT

Envy and jealousy

I said to a friend, 'I'm writing about envy at the moment'. He said, 'Good heavens, that must be so difficult for you. I can't imagine you knowing anything about envy.' That made me feel quite guilty, of course: envy was clearly something pretty sinful, something not admitted to too often. But of course I feel it sometimes, and I know that others do too. Some people envy material possessions, some envy relationships ('I wish I had a marriage like his'), or power or skills, or the apparent ability of people to obtain what they want without even trying. A husband might envy his wife's freedom and lack of responsibility; a wife might envy her husband's freedom and lack of responsibility – even in the same marriage!

A gap which needs filling

Although I know it exists, it's one of the last feelings that people talk about. Even clients in therapy for some time find it hard to admit that they envy someone. I think the reason for this difficulty must be that, to acknowledge that you're feeling envious, means you are without something that someone else has, that you are needy by comparison, and perhaps that the other person is enlarged and you are diminished and can be crushed. David finally described his feelings towards a work colleague:

'Jack gets away with murder. He just goes along being charming, never giving any aggravation, but never giving anything creative or original either. There are areas of the job which he hasn't a clue about, but he manages to get away with it. He never tells the boss what he thinks of him, though I know he despises him. He rides on the back of me and everyone else. I wake up in the middle of the night raging about it. I'm in such a stew I stay awake for hours. I used to think it was just anger at the injustice of it all, and plot how to expose him, but since I've managed to recognise it as envy I actually find it easier to deal with. When I was raging against injustice it felt as if there was something I could do to change things, but everything I wanted to do was nasty, so I couldn't. Now I see it simply as envy, it's easier somehow. I now can view it as something within myself that I can change, rather than something out there that I'm powerless really to do anything about.'

Melanie Klein, who did much to develop Freud's work in this country, saw envy as starting very young. When a baby is newborn it makes no distinction between itself and other objects, including its mother – it's as if the baby encompasses the world. Envy, she said, arises at the time that the baby first realises that the good things in life – food and cuddles from its mother – are not an integral part of its body, but actually belong to someone else, someone who can give the goodies or withhold them as she pleases. The baby begins to envy not just the fact that the mother holds the things it wants, but also that she has the power to give them or to refuse. Enough to make anyone angry, that's for sure; and, if you watch a young baby with face screwed up with rage at the fact that it's hungry and no one has instantly appeared to fill the hole, then you can see how strong an emotion envy is and how potentially destructive it can be.

Self-destructive envy

Dorothy is in a home for the elderly. Her daughter, Jill, and son-in-law and their family live only half a mile away and Jill helped to choose the home so that Dorothy could see them all regularly. But things just weren't working out. Jill visited three times a week at first, and Dorothy went to them for Sunday lunch, but the visits quickly became uncomfortable and then unbearable, and now excuses were flying fast. Dorothy continually made snide remarks to Jill or her husband about how nice it must be to have so much, and of course, with their busy social life they would always find it hard to

93

see much of her, and so on. Jill became guilty, and then cross about this; her husband was furious at Jill's reaction and at the old lady's selfishness and nastiness. The children were starting to think it wasn't worth having granny round because it made everyone so unpleasant, and she didn't even seem to enjoy seeing them anyway.

'I knew I was destroying everything I loved most,' said Dorothy. 'But I felt completely overpowered with feelings of being hard done by and angry. I couldn't think past what I didn't have, rather than what I did. Everything felt so unfair and I could only blame my daughter. Finally, another lady in the home said one day how envious she was of people who could just hop into their cars and go where they wanted. She said it so lightly, with a laugh, but it hit me very hard. I suddenly realised that I was simply envious of Jill, of her marriage and her family life. I knew that what I was doing was actually trying to destroy her pleasure, as if that would make me feel better, which of course it wouldn't. I decided to talk to Jill about it all, and, once I'd admitted to behaving so badly and the reasons I saw for it, I felt cleansed in some way. We both cried, and we've been more honest and open about things since then than I think we've been throughout our whole relationship. I've turned things round too, so now I actually feel grateful for the times I have with them, and enjoy them enormously, rather than just feeling sour at what she has.'

Recognising envy and handling it well, forgiving yourself for not being perfect, allows you to enjoy love and feel gratitude, as Dorothy found to her pleasure. Gratitude is a very mature feeling; it doesn't always flow on tap, even if little voices on our shoulder are telling us that it should. But it can come when envy fades away.

Before David accepted his emotions for what they were, he was for ever thinking of ways to get at Jack and to put a spanner in the works of his easy-going career. Undoubtedly he was putting a lot of energy into these schemes which he could more usefully have put either into his work or into trying to understand what it was he felt he lacked which Jack had, and whether there were other ways to fill it or to simply leave it behind him. He tried to think back to times when he had felt as he did now in the middle of the night. He realised that the feelings had come strongly throughout his childhood and concerned the relationship between his father and his elder brother. He was jealous of his brother, he knew that; but what he felt more strongly was envy of their easy-going way of getting along together. He had tried to be like his brother, and tried to do extra things for his father when he failed, but nothing seemed to make any difference, and the envy of something apparently so wonderful, that he could never quite achieve, left him feeling just awful. The feelings appeared to go with adulthood and marriage, but had been awakened by this similar situation at work, where his colleague could so easily relate to his boss and apparently do very little else.

'Realising that what I was missing belonged to years before allowed me to feel sadness for what I didn't have as a child, rather than spending all my energies raging against something in the present. I began to look more rationally not at what made Jack get on, but at what stopped me, and I realised that I was overdoing my critical approach and getting people's backs up. I also could see that it wasn't just to do with Jack; that actually our boss was failing to some extent as a manager. I'd never been able to see any wrong in him before. I began to concentrate much more on doing my work in the way I enjoyed for my own benefit instead of wondering what my boss would think of it. I still think Jack does get away with murder sometimes, but I can accept a bit better that there's no reason to think that the world should be just and fair. It isn't!'

Keeping parents safe

Envy is certainly destructive: it can torment you and distract you from pleasure, as it did to David, or, like Dorothy, it can cause you to get rid of something you care about and love, even though the only person to lose out might be you. On the other hand, because it creates so much anxiety, some people cope with this by idealising the person they envy most: putting them on a pedestal, out of harm's way! So David had idealised his boss and been unable to see his shortcomings; a teenager might hero-worship a pop star, longing to be at his feet, in his arms.

Children often envy their parents' power over them and, finding their angry feelings about this causes them acute anxiety, they will turn this envy into idealising them instead. So, through childhood, we see our parents as incapable of doing wrong. This is fine if, on the whole, the parents behave reasonably well towards their children; but if they punish them harshly, or dent their self-esteem with continual criticism, or abuse them, then the children have to blame themselves, not the perfect parent, and often the guilt and depression this creates goes on into their adult years. On the other hand, children with good-enough parents will gradually realise their weaknesses and failures, and the idealisation will be replaced with a more realistic picture of the world which lets them love and admire the good parts of themselves as well as the good things in their parents.

On the other hand, parents do often envy their children, not just in specific situations as Dorothy had done to her daughter Jill, but throughout their lives. They can envy them their youth and beauty, the caring that they're actually receiving, the chance they might have to do things differently and better. In *My Mother/My Self*, Nancy Friday talks about the envy and jealousy that exists in both directions between mother and daughter, but it happens just as frequently between father and son as well. It can cause the child to feel guilty of anything it achieves or acquires; to be depressed at success or to deny itself the chance of doing well. It's usually a great relief to people to realise that so much of their parents' behaviour towards them was actually to do with the envy that they felt. It takes very honest and brave parents to admit to feeling anything so unpleasant towards the child they're supposed to be nourishing and helping to succeed. But such feelings really are very normal and, if they're admitted, they lose much of their power and suddenly you find you can leave them all behind.

Three's a crowd

Envy and jealousy are related, of course. But whereas envy can exist between only two people, jealousy always concerns the tortured triangle (real or imagined). Whereas envy is to do with not having something that you want, jealousy concerns having something but being frightened that you'll lose it. Envy might be caused by a parent being very self-centred and unable to let a child feel good about itself; jealousy might be caused by a parent being unable to make the child feel secure. This may occur because the child feels that the mother or father can't be trusted, or because the parents' relationship is not well defined, so that a little boy might continue to think he had a chance to marry his mother or a girl her father. As was pointed out in Chapter 6 on guilt, children always have these yearnings at some stage and it's up to the parents to make the boundaries clear between parental love and sexual love.

But jealousy is normal and natural and so old an emotion that it appears throughout the world in myths, legends and fairy stories: look how Cinderella and Snow White suffered its vicious darts. It weaves its way in and out of the Bible too: Joseph's brothers did pretty unpleasant things to Joseph because their father favoured him; Cain killed his younger brother because he was jealous of God's preference for Abel. But it isn't always the victims we find ourselves sympathising with: many adults thinking back to reading that story as children, will recall feeling that Cain's action was understandable, even if they didn't say so at the time. Siblings in particular are extremely jealous of each other, even if neither of them may actually show it. Instead they may hide it in rather aggressive cuddles or squeeze their new sister's cheeks with an intensity that's far from affectionate. And it happens too in only children who have a younger rival around them for any length of time. We expect a lot of our children if we think they shouldn't be jealous; let's face it, it's comparable to a wife bringing home a new lover and saying to her husband: 'I know you'll be really good friends and love each other.' Children need to be given permission to express their jealous feelings verbally or in drawings, and then they are much less likely to act it out physically!

These strong feelings of jealous rage are an additional reason why the illness, accident or death of a sibling is so traumatic for children: they will often feel that they caused what happened by their wicked thoughts. Children need to be given the chance to talk about their fears and feelings of guilt over this.

Sometimes sisters and brothers manage to grow out of jealousies when they become adults, but for many it lasts much longer. I always remember being on a counselling course and talking about jealousy.

Ann, a fellow student, very mature and elegant and clearly rich, started telling us how jealous she'd been of her younger sister: all in the past tense, as if she were describing history. Within seconds she was going pink with fury as she described the lovely leather jacket her father had bought the sister last Christmas when Ann was only given a handbag. It's powerful stuff, jealousy.

Like envy, it too can be used to hurt others and to hurt yourself. Frank, always jealous of his younger brother, hurt him frequently. His mother tried to control her fury over this, but often failed and hit out at Frank. More and more he turned into the family demon, and more and more his little brother turned himself into the angel. It was as if they had to take caricatures of roles in order to make themselves as different as possible. Of course, Frank lost out in this crazy competition, because his 'bad' role wouldn't let him be nice (which he was) or do well at school (though he was very bright) or look good (although he was very handsome). Helping a friend renovate some antiques led, by chance, to Frank's starting his own business and, as his confidence grew, he was able to become all the things he'd denied over the years as well as acknowledging the love he felt for his brother. Of course, it also meant the brother could stop playing the angel!

But, as most of us know, jealousy is not confined to brothers and sisters. The type that hurts us most, that winds us up into an agonising knot, that has some of us scurrying round in the dead of night checking on whether a certain car is parked near a suspect lover's house, that makes us behave so badly at times that we can lose even a marriage that formerly had no grain of infidelity – that's jealousy of our partners.

Although all jealousy shows that we feel insecure to some degree or other, this sense of insecurity is, for most of us, kept well within tolerable bounds. We might feel ourselves getting a little uptight as we watch our partner obviously enjoying flirting with someone at a party. We might have a twinge of jealousy when we know that the other member of the business trip whom he or she is pretending disinterest about is actually a glamorous woman or man. There's nothing abnormal about that!

Nor is there anything unusual about feeling intensely, dreadfully jealous when we know, or suspect with good reason, that our partner is actually having an affair. There still seems to be some strange shadow from the Sixties which makes some people think that their partner's sexual relationships with another man or woman should be tolerated if the partner is honest and open about it. If you're in this position, you'll feel jealous: that's OK, it's normal, and I would be surprised if it wasn't almost universal. It might make you feel almost physically in pain, but pain is a sign for us to change something – a signal that you should alter aspects of your life to help relieve it.

How you tackle the pain of this rational jealousy will depend very much on the circumstances. Diana was told by her best friend that she and Don, Diana's husband, had been having an affair for the last year, and that she was now pregnant. 'I spent the day just raging,' she told me. 'I beat away at a great fat cushion for a long time, sometimes thinking it was Don and sometimes it was her. I cried non-stop and I screamed words I didn't know I knew. When Don came home he had on his naughty little boy look: the cute one that must have pleased his mother and got him off some hooks in the past. I felt much calmer after all the banging, and I realised I didn't want to talk to him at all just then. I just packed a bag and went to stay with a friend for a few days.

'I guess I was a real pain, because I went on and on, day and night, about them both. She was fantastic. She's got this wonderful Australian accent, and, after a few days of my ranting, she said to me really solemnly: "Well, Di. If you want to kill them, that's OK with me. I can be a real good liar in a witness box or out of it, so we can always cook up an alibi between us." Honestly, it was the best thing she could have said. Of course, I'd been secretly planning their murders, and her saying that gave me permission to feel murderous and yet at the same time took the feeling away. We both burst out laughing, and nothing was as bad again. I could go back and discuss things with Don and decide I didn't want the split relationship he was offering, and so we separated. I'll never really be sure whether she was joking about that murder or not!'

Irrational jealousy

Then there is the abnormal sort of jealousy, the irrational kind which makes you put unending demands on your partner, for example, that he or she constantly cares for and pays attention exclusively to you. It's the type of jealousy which makes you worry excessively whenever your partner is out of your sight, just in case he or she is, as is suspected, really enjoying passionate love with someone else. Karl behaved like this with his wife. For years she had put up with it, feeling almost flattered at first that he loved her so. As the children grew more independent, she began to anticipate a job and a little independence of her own, but he became more and more possessive, and began to make her life a misery. Eventually, she insisted that they must go for counselling or she would have to leave him.

The counsellor decided to work first just with him: he was given specific periods each day (15 minutes in the morning and evening) to feel murderously jealous if he wanted to; the rest of the day he had to use cognitive techniques of capturing irrational negative thoughts in his diary and replacing them with positive rational alternatives (see the diary in Figure 4, p. 66). He and the counsellor went over role-plays to help him deal with situations where he was jealous, and he imagined them while he was relaxing and, when he found himself becoming jealous, he substituted disappointment and sadness instead. He went over the 'Worst Scenario' technique (see Chapter 7, p. 90), of what would happen if his wife really had an affair, and how he'd cope with this. As his wife began to attend the sessions, they agreed each week that she should spend progressively longer times away from the house, and he should use the techniques he was now familiar with to handle her absences.

One day, trying to remember whether he had felt like this as a child, he realised that, while his father was away at war, his mother had taken a lover. He was only four, but he knew now that he knew then. It was a very important experience for him, recalling his feelings of jealousy then on his father's behalf and also on his own.

Sometimes people use irrational jealousy as the only way they know to show affection for their partner, and they may need to recognise that there are other ways to do this. For example, Maggie and Paul came for help because her jealousy was spoiling their social life. It turned out, however, that Paul showed no affection to her – he didn't know how – and so every eyebrow twitch or indication of polite interest he showed to other women became loaded with meaning for Maggie. She needed that for herself.

Basically, with both jealousy and envy, the monster within us loses its power when we confess, whether to ourselves or to someone else, that that is what we're feeling. Once we've done this, we can start trying to understand and to find other ways of trusting and loving.

Things to do about envy and jealousy

* *Try substituting 'envy' or 'jealousy' for the anger and indignation that you're feeling. Do they fit?*

* *Forgive yourself for feeling envious or jealous: that will take away a lot of the anger that's attached. Talk about it if you can.*

* *If you feel envy, check what it suggests is missing in your life: is it appreciation, or friendship, or power? If it's merely wealth, ask yourself what wealth would mean to you.*

* *When you're feeling envious or jealous, try to recall when you've felt like this before. Write it down and add to it over time. Is there a pattern? If so, decide to let go of the past.*

* *Is someone spoiling things for you because of their envy? If so, don't accept it or feel guilty or think that you should fail to please them. It's their problem, not yours.*

* *Accept that jealousy and anger amongst siblings, and over actual infidelity in adults, is absolutely normal. You don't have to be polite!*

* *If jealousy is irrational and spoiling an otherwise good relationship, work on the 'Worst Scenario' and how you'd cope.*

✳ *Capture envious and jealous thoughts in a diary and teach yourself to substitute more rational ones.*

✳ *Work at accepting more and more independence in your partner and discover you can survive alone.*

CHAPTER NINE

Feeling shame

Naomi was a mature student. One day in lectures, she was asked to come to the board to draw a diagram to illustrate the lecturer's point. As she stepped up on to the dais she broke wind loudly. The class murmured and some people tittered and she dropped the chalk and ran out of the room, out of the university and home. She didn't return for weeks, not until a group of fellow students came to visit her and told her as many of their own embarrassing and shaming experiences that they could think of. In the end they had her laughing too, and at that point she had to admit that what she'd done was by no means the end of the world, and she could live with it. Once she'd gone through the ordeal of attending her first lecture again, her emotional turmoil was over.

Shame is an awful feeling. It seizes you up, it makes you cringe. People talk about it immobilising them; they feel scorned and small, and want to hide; their tongues get tied in knots and their minds go blank. They are totally aware of themselves and they will often blush or stammer or sweat. Inside they feel they're raging and crying. It's one of the most powerful feelings of all.

In fact the word shame comes from an Indo-European root (*skem*) which means 'to hide' and a hide is also a skin or a cover. It's an old word and it's an old, old feeling. Adam and Eve were said to suffer shame after they'd tasted the apple: they instantly became aware of themselves and started rummaging for fig leaves to cover the bits that worried them. Certainly shame still has many links with our bodies, and especially with our sexuality, and is almost always to do with some sort of situation where we feel exposed to someone more

103

powerful than ourselves. When we feel ashamed there's always that Other there to haunt us. What is unusual about shame is that society almost seems to want us to feel it. If I don't feel shame I'm likely to be regarded as pretty wicked: there's nothing so shaming as to be told, with a tut-tut-tut, that you're shameless!

Scientists see society's opinion and our subservience to it as the key to the origins of shame; and the pressure shame creates they see as a normal and necessary part of the evolution of social behaviour, not just in us but in other animals too. Shame plays a role similar to embarrassment and feeling shy in underlying many of our normal social interactions. As shyness, it starts when we are very young indeed: almost as soon as infants are properly aware that other people exist. Those who study animals see it as causing the behaviour – the cringing and making yourself small – that lets the more powerful Other (lion, labrador, baboon or boss) overlook you, not get mad at you, because you're insignificant, absolutely no threat at all. Well, that might be OK for dogs, but we humans don't like being made to feel small, and so shame in us can get muddled up with ferocious anger and also sometimes with guilt.

It's different from guilt, however, because in guilt the Other party is not strong and humiliating as happens in shame, but has, in your view, been hurt in some way by you. You have to feel responsible to feel guilty, but you feel helpless when you're ashamed. When you're feeling guilty, no one but you may know what you've done or haven't done, but when you're ashamed someone has always seen you in a way you wish they hadn't. Moreover, people who feel guilty usually want to talk about it, to confess; those who feel ashamed don't want anyone ever to know.

Shy, embarrassed or ashamed

Shyness, embarrassment and shame differ, but mainly in degree. Shyness is something almost everyone has experienced at some time or other: a recent British survey found 80% of people admitted to being or having been shy, and probably the other 20% felt too shy to admit it! It only happens when you're actually with people (especially ones you don't know), whereas shame is triggered by memory as much as anything: even as an adult I remember cringing for years over minor childhood humiliations. Although the emotions in embarrassment and shyness are not so strongly felt as in shame, they can still affect your life considerably.

Annette said she'd suffered from embarrassment all her adult life. 'The problem is that whenever I am in conversation with someone, especially a man, I find myself beginning to blush. I've changed my job to one where I work alone, although I'd much rather enjoy one that's sociable, and I've given up music lessons, despite really wanting to learn, because I turned crimson every time the teacher spoke to me. And then he'd say, you don't need to blush, and that made it worse.'

This constellation of feelings – shyness, embarrassment and shame – occurs more in situations with the opposite sex, as Annette knows. It's also extremely common. Most psychologists now are seeing these outward signs as simply a way of letting some 'dominant' person know that we are not going to be any trouble to them – they don't have to harm us or ridicule us. Like many of the other emotions we've talked about, our physiology hasn't caught up with the 1990s: it doesn't know about equality and things like that!

The American psychologist Albert Ellis, however, sees shyness and embarrassment as just an excuse to stop you making a relationship. He says it's usually based on an irrational belief such as 'I must please every attractive man/woman I meet, otherwise I'm pretty useless!' You could test this out by telling yourself you don't have to please anyone but yourself; if you believe it (and obviously it's true), then it should certainly take the pressure off new encounters.

The other point about embarrassment and shame is that they involve us in imagining what the other person sees: it's not Annette's cheeks going pink that causes the problem; it's her imagining the man's view of her embarrassment that makes her squirm. So on the one hand they're caused by our feeling weak or humiliated, but on the other hand we feel that in some way we are the centre of attention, at least for that one person whom we see as dominant.

Other-consciousness

So this gives us other ways to tackle the shyness and embarrassment that, even when mild, may nevertheless keep us, like Annette, from enjoying a full life. First, we have to keep reminding ourselves that feeling shy and blushing, for example, isn't abnormal, but just an everyday part of social functioning; in fact, most people actually find blushing very attractive, something to be cherished.

The other method – one useful for all feelings of self-consciousness – is to realise that we are very rarely the centre of attention that we think we are. We are not so important, not so fascinating , not always in someone else's thoughts. Instead we must force ourselves to see that, just as we're always wondering what people are thinking about us, those people are wondering just the same thing: what is she/he/my boss/my hero thinking about me? Once you realise this, it takes the spotlight off you and swings it round to the other person. You remember to tell yourself that everyone in the room feels a little bit shy, and some of them are longing to hide away somewhere; you begin to concentrate on others instead of yourself. Instead of being self-conscious you become other-conscious.

Peter had failed to get two jobs even though he was very well qualified for both of them. 'I just fell apart in the interview basically. I knew I was blushing and mumbling, and when they asked me things that I had thought about a lot, my mind just went blank. All I could think of was whether they could see I was sweating, whether my tie was right, what they must think of me. The more I thought this, the worse I felt. I still shrivel up, just thinking of that row of men and women watching me.'

Before his next interview he taught himself a variety of ways to get in control. He learned to relax and practised doing this in a variety of situations he usually found difficult. If he found himself sweating, he told himself quickly, 'Thank goodness my body's behaving normally' as often as he needed. Most importantly, he trained himself in other-consciousness: each day he set himself the task of noticing and commenting on something about the person he was talking to. At the beginning, this person could be anyone, but gradually he made himself do it with people he saw as dominant or frightening –

those who made him nervous so he felt like blushing. They might be small comments, like: 'You're looking tired/pleased with yourself/ tanned/cross'. Or they might be ones that required him to give quite a lot of attention to the Other, to check out how things really were with him or her; for example, 'You seemed to be at odds with X in this morning's meeting', or 'You really enjoy this sort of challenge, don't you?'

When his next interview came he practised his relaxation in the waiting room, and frequently checked his body over throughout the meeting, dropping his shoulders whenever he felt them going tense. He focused his attention partly on the questions but also on the four people interviewing him: how they looked, what sort of people they were, and, most important, what was their relationship to each other: who was trying to impress whom with clever questions. He found this not only seemed to take the pressure off him, but also gave him a better understanding of what each of them wanted from him, so he was better able to answer the questions. He got the job.

A cycle of shame

Shame may be a normal feeling and perhaps, as the scientists say, a useful curb on the real excesses of behaviour, but it can nevertheless be very upsetting and even damaging to individuals if they hang on to it for any length of time. What is worse, if the events which caused it also involved hurt and humilation, then it will be linked to anger and quite possibly carried forward in a cycle of shaming behaviour.

For example, Eric sought help after his teaching skills were questioned by a superior at the special school where they were both employed. He was unusually short, about five foot two, but very smart with clothes that looked almost like a uniform. He said how worried he felt about all the bullying that went on in the school between the boys, and the word 'bullying' cropped up a number of times as he spoke – a film he'd seen on TV, a cousin whom he'd learnt had been sexually abused, and so on. His own way of curbing school bullies was to 'cuddle' them till they stopped. His father, he said, was a wonderful man – tall, strong, a very senior policeman, and a real inspiration to him.

On a suggestion that he might be very worried about being a bully himself, he broke down and he said he knew he was, that he had dreadful rages against the boys, and he felt quite murderous to them at times. Shortly after this, he talked about his father again, and this time there emerged a picture of a particularly cruel man who had humiliated his small son at every opportunity he had. Instead of needing to pass on his shame and rage at these dreadful childhood experiences, he could now face the truth and work on that, rather than pretending that his problems were concerned with something as superficial as teaching skills. The possible passing on of shame and humiliation makes it an emotion we really need to deal with as soon as it is experienced, not just for our sakes but for our family's and for society as a whole.

Talking about it

As Eric discovered, actually facing the shaming situation in all its detail, is the only way to begin to deal with it. At eighteen Lisa still felt dreadful whenever she thought about an incident in her childhood. When she was six and had just learnt to read properly, her mother gave her a book of Hans Christian Andersen stories, and she read them avidly. When she'd finished 'The Emperor's New Clothes', however, she remembers feeling quite horrified: how terrible to be naked, and in front of all those people. She went next door and told the little boy there about the story, omitting the fact that the emperor was actually naked. With the promise of magic clothes, she got him to take off his trousers, and so gave herself her first sight of a naked male.

Although it's actually very normal for children to try to find out how the other sex looks, all the parents treated it as a major disgrace, and the whispers and tight lips hung about her still: if they thought she was shameless, they were certainly very wrong. As a teenager, she broke off relationships with boyfriends almost before they'd begun, just in case they got fresh. This went on until at last, twelve years later, she was able to talk openly about it in a women's group, and to hear everyone else's funny stories of early inquisitiveness about sex. Then it all shrank into proportion.

FEELING SHAME

There's remarkably little written about shame, and I suspect that this is because we all feel it – all we writers and psychologists and helpers – we all have our own areas that make us cringe and writing about it reminds us of these. But this silence is the very thing that makes the feeling of shame continue: we all think we're the only one that this has happened to because we all keep so quiet about it.

This has been the experience of the many women and some men who were sexually abused as children and young adults and who, with all the publicity of the last few years, have finally decided to find ways to deal with the torment that this experience still causes in their adult lives. The basic emotion of sexual abuse is shame – the terrible exposure of little boys and girls to every sort of humiliation that their fathers or brothers or lodgers, or even mothers and sisters, can think of. Their stories, if and when they finally manage to tell them, are far more harrowing than most of us, thank goodness, could ever imagine.

Of course, they also feel enormous anger and many turn their shame into guilt, feeling that they were in some way to blame for what happened to them. I think this is because guilt implies that you have some power, that you seduced the abuser in some way, and so is a less terrible emotion than the real fact that you were totally help-less, a victim at some dominant person's mercy.

As with all other less severe forms of shame and embarrassment, the only way to start dealing with childhood abuse (or, for that matter, adult abuse like rape) is to start by admitting in accurate detail just what happened to you. People will often use soft words and half truths about what really went on, and they need to be encouraged to spell it out just as it was. This is usually the first exercise in the increasing number of groups being set up by health authorities and social services to help this hidden population who have been silent for so long.

Maria told me: 'It was dreadful speaking out like that. My voice was just a whisper and there were words I couldn't say at first. But gradually the therapist and the other women gave me the courage to speak a little louder and say a little more. When I'd finally told, for the first time ever, it was like lifting a great weight off me. It was only a beginning of the healing, but it had to happen before I could go on.'

If you feel you should join one of these groups, but there's quite a waiting list, or if you feel you're not quite ready, then at least begin by writing out what happened to you, or speaking it on to a tape. Again, go into as much detail as you can. The whole exercise is about facing up to the reality. Write down too the physical sensations that you have as you do the exercise, and any other emotions that well up, like guilt and anger. Try to explore those in the same way. If you want you can write a letter about it to the abuser, not to send, but to relieve some of the anger that you feel. Other ways of dealing with the anger that attaches to shame are described in Chapter 4 (p. 45).

As with other less powerful emotions like embarrassment, someone who has been abused in this way still feels some link with the person who did it: they usually imagine that they are in that person's thoughts frequently. Learning to realise that you are probably irrelevant and unimportant to him or her is one of the first steps towards letting go of the past. This is why you don't send the letter. Your aim in these exercises is to get things off your chest and to let go of the past by doing this, not to stir up a new, if different, relationship with the abuser. Letting go is the hardest part, but the most useful.

Childhood abuse needs professional help. You might get some way on your own, but it's bound to be disturbing. So don't be afraid to go and ask your doctor where you can get specialised help, and don't try the exercises above unless you feel you're bursting with pain and emotion. The help offered might be a group of others with experiences like your own, or it might be one-to-one therapy. If this has happened to you, you're used to keeping it all to yourself and used to the fact that no one in the past listened to you or helped you with it, especially not at the time when someone might have rescued you. It's important, however, not to let this past history stop you from seeking help now. You're going to begin to learn how to leave your past behind you.

Things to do about embarrassment and shame

❋ *Realise that shame is a biological way to keep us in check. Decide that, while you can't do anything about your out-dated physiology, you can decide not to let it be the arbiter of how you feel in the future.*

110

❋ *Recognise any negative thoughts (for example, 'Everyone will think I'm a fool/disgusting/stupid/weak') and challenge them with something more rational.*

❋ *Realise you're not the centre of attention or constantly in the shamer's thoughts. That way you can leave your shame behind.*

❋ *Stop concentrating on yourself, and become Other-conscious.*

❋ *Talk about embarrassing or shaming events in detail to someone whom you can trust (I know it's hard when you've been really hurt to trust anyone, but it's worth the risk). Any bits of the account you leave out will go on making you squirm, so try to make it as full as possible.*

❋ *If talking is too difficult for some reason, then write it all down or speak it into a tape recorder.*

❋ *Use the exercises in Chapter 4 (p. 54) to deal with any anger that's still around.*

❋ *Seek help if your memories are really painful. I know it's hard to believe that someone can help, especially when you've been so careful to guard your secret, but eventually the relief will be worth it.*

CHAPTER TEN

Feeling selfish

When you're deciding to do something for yourself, do you ever hear a voice which says, 'You're just selfish through and through. You think of no one but yourself'? For some people, such accusations rule everything they do as adults; to them, acting for their own benefit, not always being considerate of others, is out of the question, driven out very early so that, even when they long to be cared for, or be assertive, self-interest is prohibited.

'I know it doesn't do my family any good for me never to think of myself,' said June, 'And I won't deny I get very grumpy about doing everything for everyone else. But if ever someone does something for me, I feel so uncomfortable and guilty, I wish they wouldn't. It's not worth it. It's like presents: I love giving presents and part of me hopes I'll get something wonderful back. But then if I'm given something nice I feel so guilty. I worry like mad that it might be better than I've given them. I get in such a stew. It's really better to be the giver, I think.'

June is in a dilemma: if she does everything for others she feels angry and uncared for, and if she treats herself or if others do things for her, then she feels at best uncomfortable, at worst guilty and selfish. Women, in particular, feel like this; perhaps because, until the present generation at least, their mothers brought them up more to serve than to be served. Taking care of number one, a very natural and important urge, was often smothered by a lavish dollop of guilt by mothers who themselves had very often had little in the way of generous care given to them. Some people see this as mothers preparing their daughters realistically for the world; others argue that it

112

concerns envy within the mother/daughter relationship, an envy which leads to stopping the daughter from enjoying more than the mother had herself. It would be good to think that this ladling out of guilt over any behaviour which smacks of self-love, self-care or self-interest is reducing all the time with the greater assertiveness and freedom of young women today. We'll have to wait and see whether or not this really happens.

Finding power where you can

But also selfless behaviour does carry with it a certain feeling of power. You can almost hear this in June's words: she feels more comfortable, more in control, if she is doing the giving than if someone else is – if people are dependent on her rather than she on them. Again, feminists have pointed out that this type of behaviour – slaving away over a hot stove, never asking for help or refusing it if it's given, is the only area of power that women had. The kitchen and domestic tools were made as mysterious by some women as the office and the motor car were by some men.

But men can use selfless behaviour in the powerful way as well. In Chapter 3, on anxiety, I talked about some women with agoraphobia having husbands who did everything for them to save them going outside their homes. Karen, for example, had a corner shop which she'd run for years while her husband worked in a factory. When he was made redundant, she spent more and more time at the back, letting him run the shop and get in supplies. She became nervous of driving and finally of going out into the shop if customers were there. When the doctor referred her for help, it quickly became apparent that, as her problems improved and she began to play her role in the shop once again, her husband grew anxious and unhappy. Seen alone, he gradually talked about his wretchedness and feelings of powerlessness on being made redundant, and the importance to him of having an area where he felt in charge and in control. Marital counselling let them learn to find the ways of both giving and receiving, being dependent and independent, that every partnership should strive for.

Consuming passions

Another form of 'selfish' behaviour is linked to greediness. It occurs in compulsive eating, for example, and bulimia (where people can eat a cupboard full of food and then force themselves to vomit), in alcoholism and in compulsive shopping, where people spend, spend, spend to give themselves brief lifts, much as another person will use drink. Most of these people describe a feeling of emptiness and use the heavy consumption of food or drink or spending to provide themselves with a temporary high, which is inevitably followed by a low and which gradually produces more and more problems. Guilt is very much a part of this behaviour: they are in fact driven on in their addiction partly by a need to block out the selfish, guilty and greedy feelings they experience.

Mike had a mother who, all through his childhood, did 'good works', helping at the church and with the guides, and any neighbours who were in need always knew they could rely on her. But she gave very little to her son. His father had left home when he was young, and he had no brothers or sisters. He remembered always having to let himself in after school, the emptiness of the house, doing the washing up from breakfast and getting himself a snack for tea. His mother would rush in and out, and he felt constantly unwanted and in the way. Once she told him, clearly deeply ashamed: 'You were a mistake. I wouldn't have married your father but for you.'

Not surprisingly Mike grew up feeling pretty selfish even to be alive. He went into social work in a very deprived area of London, married a girl with considerable problems of her own, and gradually began to drink and then to gamble. 'The drinking took the guilt away, and the gambling felt like the most wonderful exciting selfish thing I could imagine. Before that, my most selfish act was fulfilling a childhood fantasy by having a whole tin of peaches and Carnation milk all to myself, and I'd only done that once! But I had to have the drink to control the guilt, and so things pretty quickly began to go out of control. When my marriage went wrong I ended up in psychotherapy, thank goodness, and was able to make links between these bursts of behaviour and what it was like to have this apparently selfless mother who gave me nothing. It was so difficult ever to express a need, and I still have to force myself. I've made myself realise that there's a whole world of little acts which I can do and which give me pleasure, which are between being totally selfless and splurging everying in gambling, and I'm enjoying discovering more. I try a new treat out every day! And I've begun to assert myself at work.'

Finding occasional self-interested behaviour difficult might be caused because we feel we don't deserve it; because our parents led us to believe that looking after our own interests and pleasure was always wrong. It may also come about because you had to act as if you didn't need your parents' special care because they were so busy or so troubled themselves. This might not be like Mike's mother, where her actions were clearly dealing with some need of her own and were also decidedly cruel to her young son; it can also occur where the parents are poor and have to work hard, long hours, so that they're either absent or tired. Or because one of them is depressed and so 'absent' in one sense and 'ill' in another. In these cases the child will often feel guilty about expressing any wish or need of its own because it knows that really its parents are unable to act in any other way. Sometimes this can be even tougher for the child than where he or she can actually feel 'legitimately' angry with a parent because they're clearly being ill-treated.

Many of you reading this will, like me, have to work and will come home tired, and home life will inevitably be busy with everyone mucking in. There is nothing wrong with this in itself. It's only a problem if children are not given the chance to do something just for themselves occasionally, to luxuriate in laziness now and then, to treat themselves as important and worth while, which they'll be able to do if they're treated that way by their parents. It won't be a problem either if they are able to express the other feelings they have about having to help a great deal, not seeing as much of their parents as they'd like, having to be patient and understanding for much of the time. They are bound to feel annoyed at this, and being able to express it and be listened to without their mother or father getting upset or cross, because they too feel guilty, is one of the best things we can do for our children.

The other reason we can get stuck into constantly selfless behaviour as adults is that it's often rewarded in children, and when children do behave in this uncharacteristically generous way most of the time, it can be quite shocking if they suddenly assert themselves. Judith went to a convent school. When the nuns handed round oranges after dinner she would always take the smallest, although she did like oranges. The nuns became very proud of her and would use her to demonstrate just how unselfish some people could be. One day when a visiting bishop came to the school, the nun took the plate of oranges first to Judith. Among several of average size, there was one enormous one and one very small one. The nun was smiling at the bishop in pride before she realised that Judith had snatched the big one from the plate. She still remembers that with intense pleasure and only a vestige of guilt!

Addicted to helping

Of course we don't want everyone to be totally selfish all the time; it would be an awful world if that was the case. But there is a legitimate level of self-interest which includes caring for yourself, doing things for yourself and expressing your own needs to others. If you really find it hard to act in your own self-interest at least now and then, it can lead to unhappiness for you and also affect those around you. June, for example, recognised that doing everything for her family was not doing them any good: they would grow up dependent and unsure and possibly unbearably selfish. Mike, the social worker, also realised that he wasn't doing the best for his wife or his clients by putting himself out to try to solve all their problems. During therapy he learnt to let go of a little of this overwhelming sense that he must make things better.

'I think part of it came from feeling that my mother's unhappiness was something to do with me: if I hadn't been born she wouldn't have had to marry my father. Also of course, it felt clear to me as a child (and as an adult) that my father didn't want me – that I'd not been enough to keep him around. It made me want to make everything right for other people that I couldn't make right for them. I'm sure that's why I became a social worker in the first place! But gradually I had to realise that I was behaving in quite a controlling way to all these people I was supposed to be helping. I think I've been much more use to them since I began to let them go, and encourage them to realise that they could do things for themselves. The same with my wife: I didn't realise how mad she was at me for keeping her dependent, for doing everything for her all the time. We're not out of the woods, but things are much better now I'm allowing it to be more of a partnership.'

I'm sure Mike's right in thinking that being a social worker is no coincidence. Psychoanalysts have talked about the 'Helping Profession' Syndrome – the need for people to go into jobs where they can help others in order unconsciously to try and make good something at which they feel they'd failed as a child. Some nurses, doctors, therapists of all kinds, social workers and psychologists may fall into this trap of thinking they were not up to scratch as children, and so have to keep on helping now they're adults. But it's not just the workers: Robin Norwood in her excellent book *Women Who Love Too Much*, has pointed out how often women will fall into this trap by continually making relationships with men with problems – alcoholics, disabled, gay, troubled in some way – anyone who they can try to change, improve or help.

Norwood treats this need to help as an addiction to problems in just the same way as someone might need drugs or alcohol or gambling. She recommends abstinence from this helping/controlling behaviour so that the partner can learn to help himself, and a self-help group of similar 'addicts' to give support when she feels herself urged to provide assistance once more, or to start a new relationship with yet another troubled man. Any woman married to an alcoholic whom she's spent years trying to reform should realise that his only hope of changing is if she gives up trying to help: that's what Al Anon, the organisation for the relatives of alcoholics, advise, and it's very clear to me that this is right. Of course, it's not just women who suffer in this way. Mike had married a woman with considerable problems herself, and was drawn into therapy when the marriage became rocky and he was beginning to form a relationship with another woman who had been abused as a child. It was his courage at letting himself see the beginnings of a pattern that led to change.

So being selfish sometimes, and certainly not all-helpful and self-sacrificing, is clearly very healthy. Apart from the controlling behaviour discussed above, people who deny their own needs can become martyrly in ways discussed in the chapter on guilt. Like June, they both want other people to help and give to them (and they feel envious of them and angry that they don't), but they also feel uncomfortable when they do. Others who find it hard to assert their needs may resort to illness behaviour, as if the only way they can legitimately express their needs is if they're ill. Often people have told me that the only time they remember their parents being loving and attentive was when they were sick in bed: then they would have all the comfort and concern they wanted but never liked to ask for from busy or distracted mothers and fathers.

Asserting yourself

We hear a lot nowadays about how to be assertive, and classes are given on the subject in every city. Originally only women attended, but now they form part of courses for managers and doctors and every other group you could think of. It seems that not being able to ask for what you want is a huge problem in this country. What you learn in assertion workshops are ways of recognising what you need and asking for it, and ways of saying no when you really don't want to do something, instead of saying yes and then fuming silently at the person who asked you. It isn't to do with learning how to be aggressive: it might be no more than being able to say 'Would you mind closing the window, please' instead of shivering with cold; or repeating your request over and over when you're returning faulty goods to an aggressive salesman. It's about gaining the courage to recognise that you have the right to something, or to refuse something, and insisting – as quietly and as often as you like – that you are heard.

You can practise assertion and being 'selfish' by keeping a diary and setting yourself one assertive remark or demand and one treat each day, just for you. The treats or 'selfish' acts might be having a cream cake or a long lounging bath, setting time aside for a hobby or a small holiday, buying a piece of equipment that will make life easier, and so on. The assertive remarks may be as little as saying 'I'm feeling tired today' (daring to express your own feelings) right through to asking a neighbour to turn down their television or cut their hedge or stop parking in your space. Try writing down all the things you'd really like to say to people, but don't feel you've got the right. Put them in a hierarchy, start with the easiest and work your way up. If you find yourself shrinking away, ask what you have to lose: is it easier to feel angry with someone who isn't doing something, than have him or her perhaps feel cross with you for asking? If it is, accept that this is your choice and change things if you want.

Asking for help

Finally, people occasionally find it hard to be even selfish enough to recognise that the unhappiness they're feeling is understandable in terms of their life history or what is happening to them now. Sometimes you have the right to feel depressed just as you have the right to feel angry or to succeed at something: it's not selfish to acknowledge feeling in this way. Yes, I know half the world is starving and you're financially OK in comparison, but honestly you still have the right to feel miserable sometimes.

Further, if you are feeling stuck in your selfless, non-assertive behaviour or in your depression, then realise that this will also be stopping you from seeking help. Many people who go for help to psychologists, psychotherapists or counsellors begin by saying they shouldn't be here, they don't deserve it, they're not poorly enough, there must be lots of people far worse off than them. They come late for appointments, miss appointmtents or give up coming long before they should. They say after two appointments, 'Thank you very much. You've been so helpful. I'm much better now!' Part of this is to do with being afraid of expressing something of what they feel – their anger, their sadness, their fears – but it is also to do with the very problem itself, the inability to dare to think that someone might care for them, help them; the feeling that being 'selfish' enough to ask for this, perhaps on a regular basis, is very wrong and something they simply don't deserve. If you feel like that, realise how much it's affecting your whole life and decide to change right now.

119

Things to do to assert yourself

❋ *Ask yourself if you actually get what you want – at work, with friends and relations, with neighbours and shopkeepers, with hobbies. What do you want emotionally? What do you want sexually? Write down a list of what you really want and decide how you're going to tackle each item. Keep a diary.*

❋ *Give yourself treats, tiny and large. Observe how you feel. Does your guilt go down over time?*

❋ *Make yourself express one feeling to someone else every day.*

❋ *Think about how much you do for others. Is it really best for them? Do you really feel relaxed and at ease about doing it, or is it tied up with some resentment? Ask them how they feel about it; tell them they can be honest.*

❋ *Join an assertion workshop: if it's good it should be fun.*

❋ *If you can see that your relationships form a pattern – that you always go for someone who needs your help – then decide to let go of this urge to make things right for someone else. You will often need support to do this, but recognising it is more than half the battle.*

❋ *If you're feeling low or stuck in some selfless, unassertive pattern, accept that you have the right to ask for help to get you out. If you do seek professional help, recognise that, if you start missing appointments or coming late or thinking you should stop, this is just a symptom of the problem.*

CHAPTER ELEVEN

Feeling OK

It takes courage to change. You need courage even to recognise enough of what's happening to you to realise that change would be a good thing. If you make determined efforts to improve your life and to bring yourself peace and pleasure, this should surely earn nothing but admiration, from others and from yourself. Change should, therefore, be a reward in itself – once we have a glimmer that hope and help are possible, then we will inevitably forge ahead. Won't we? But there can be pitfalls on the way: sometimes other people might dig them for you, but often you can be very energetic and do that all by yourself!

However miserable people feel, however guilty or imprisoned with fear, however much they long to do something self-centred and fun, nevertheless they still at some point may 'decide', unconsciously, not to change. Sometimes this resistance comes before they've done more than put a toe in the water of a new life (or read more than the opening pages of a book like this); sometimes it comes much later, when they are really beginning to change and to notice how much better things are. Why, after such possibilities are glimpsed or even experienced, why do they then turn their back on the chance of feeling OK, even of experiencing moments of real pleasure and joy?

Why make things worse than they are?

Many people decide not to start to change or not to go on once they've begun because of a fear that they will uncover something awful, dig up some dreadful buried feeling or knowledge that they didn't know they had, go quite out of control. If this feeling is very strong and disturbing, then decide to get help to change rather than trying to do it on your own. But in any case, do remember that nothing can be created that isn't there already. If you don't feel OK, then chances are that helping yourself to understand this, recognising what you're denying or repressing, unravelling the feelings that you're having, and starting to find new ways of expressing yourself, can only help you.

If you find you're telling yourself 'There's no point raking up the past', remember that, where feelings are concerned, the past is the present. If you say 'I can understand why X behaved as he/she did when he/she hurt me', remember that understanding is only part of the process; getting the feeling out (not necessarily to the people concerned) may also be essential. If you catch yourself saying, 'I never feel angry/jealous/envious/afraid', remember that all feelings are a normal part of our minds and bodies, and it would be very unusual if you didn't experience them occasionally. If you do actually feel them but deny them, you are denying a part of yourself.

'I'll lose things if I change'

People who stop changing once they've begun very often do this because they recognise, often without realising it, that they'll lose something by becoming healthy again. For example, someone who is very angry may want to hold on to that anger for a while longer because it makes them feel powerful, or because it means they can go on attacking someone they feel hurt them. One woman said to me, 'I'm sorry, I'm not giving up my anger at him yet; it's too soon to let him off the hook.' Well, that's OK, especially if you recognise what you're doing. But she needed also to see that she was holding on to her anger at a cost – almost certainly at a physical cost, and perhaps at an emotional one too . For example, when a relationship ends bitterly, some people hang on to their anger so they won't become sad at what they've lost. But it's only when you do become sad that you can start to let go of the past and to move on; it's only then that you can have any chance of making good relationships in the future rather than having the shadow of your former partner hovering over you.

I've spoken before about holding on to selflessness, even to the point of becoming a martyr, because that too keeps you powerful. So make sure you're not stopping yourself from changing because you like to have people dependent just on you. On the other hand, you may find that, by changing yourself, other people around you are changing too. In a family situation or between a couple, this is almost inevitable, and sometimes it can mean that everyone feels uncomfortable for a time. If, for example, you have been depressed and housebound for quite a while, when you begin to become more cheerful and more active, other people in the family who might have enjoyed their roles as being the selfless carers, are going to lose something of that control and are going to feel perhaps a little anxious themselves.

Similarly, if you were someone who always gave in to other people's demands, starting to be strong and more assertive is bound to affect other people you relate to. But don't presume it will affect them negatively. In the long run, it will usually let them change for the better too: who knows, they may already feel guilty about always being overbearing! If it did ever come to the crunch and you felt you'd lose someone unless you changed back again to your old self quick smart, then surely you need to look hard and question such a relationship and answer honestly whether it's really best for you or whether it's part of what's wrong.

Finally, it may be that you feel you only get love and attention and friendship when you are poorly or if you behave in a certain way. For example, if you belong to a self-help group just for people with anorexia or phobias, are you able to stay (and would you want to stay) once you get better? If not, then you need to make sure this is not the only support you have or you are likely to stay thin or scared just to be part of the club! Another example is in children and young people who only get attention or treats if they misbehave. Think about the child in the supermarket: if he screams because he wants a sweet, he might get a smack first, but he will often get a sweet too. If he doesn't scream he doesn't get a sweet. Or the adolescent girl whose brother or sister is behaving abominably and getting so much attention (from parents, teachers, social workers, psychiatrists), whereas she gets none.

You need to remember whether these were patterns you recognise from when you were young, and whether they now make you able to ask for care only when things are bad. Perhaps it means you need a constant crisis, or perhaps you feel that being healthy will actually keep some of the good things away. Work out or recognise just what you might 'lose' by feeling good and find ways that you can substitute other things as you begin to change.

Feeling you don't deserve to change

For some of you who are feeling guilty or ashamed or depressed, you might decide that you should cling on to your pain and unhappiness because it's a fitting punishment. If this feeling lasts any length of time (that is, if it isn't an understandable reaction to a recent event), chances are its origins date back many years. Perhaps to your childhood where you were made to feel a burden, a 'mistake', or always in the wrong, the family problem. Perhaps to a marriage, present or ended, where your partner has needed to make you feel small in order to make himself or herself feel OK. A woman wrote to me once saying that her husband of forty years would shortly retire and that she felt so guilty since she realised she was dreading it because of the way he always put her down, both in public and in private. I had the mental picture of a tiny man (one with a tiny self-esteem) standing on the curled-up back of his wife for forty years, using her diminished strength and size to make himself feel bigger.

If your self-esteem has been crushed in this way, by parents or by partners, then you may feel as if you don't deserve to feel happy at all, and that enjoying yourself is not part of your lot in life. If you find yourself thinking this, first decide where the feeling comes from. Who gave you such an unreasonable and irrational thought in the first place? Whose is the voice you hear saying it? Now try to find some challenges for it. They might be:

✽ *I don't have to deserve something in order to do it and enjoy it.*

124

✱ *I am not helping myself or those close to me by always staying this way.*

✱ *I am not such a powerful being that I am the one to decide whether I should be punished or not.*

✱ *I am a human being and so I can feel all things including happiness.*

✱ *Other people can let go of old feelings that don't belong now. It may be slow, but I can do it too.*

✱ *What have I got to lose?*

The answer to the last question is that you have nothing to lose other than the guilt, the shame, the depression itself. If you're religious, realise that it's not up to you to decide you're not worth forgiving. Nor are you so special that you can't forgive yourself. You're ordinary like me, capable of doing good things and of doing bad things, just like everyone else.

Recognising good things when they happen

When you've felt low for some time it can be quite difficult to see that things are getting better. This may be because you're setting your targets much too high – giving yourself huge steps to achieve rather than lots of small ones – or it may be that you're so used to seeing things under a shadow of fear or guilt or shame that you don't recognise the brighter feelings when they happen. Sometimes it's useful, if you feel nothing's changing, to turn your whole emphasis around and to begin looking for only the exceptions to the rule – only the times when the guilt didn't come, the sadness lifted, the fear went away. It might only be for a minute or it might have been for a day or a month. Get yourself relaxed and think yourself back into that exceptional feeling. Notice what you were doing, thinking, and so on. Remember the feeling well so that next time it happens you won't overlook it, but will go on with whatever seems to be making it happen. This way you can start to build on change.

Give yourself permission to be with people who laugh and joke, and don't hold back on laughing too. Don't ration yourself in this but remember too that, just as feeling OK, feeling joyful and confident is normal, so is feeling sad, envious, angry, and all the rest. Once you begin to change, you will still experience all the other feelings – just like everyone else does. Remember, for instance, that if you wake up feeling miserable or anxious, so do the rest of us. We all have our 'off days', we all feel more irritable on some occasions than others. It doesn't mean that you're going to plummet back down to where you were. It's just a normal useful sign that you should attend to, so use it as a chance to check things out. Ask, for example:

✳ *Are you looking after yourself (having enough sleep, early nights, exercise, keeping low on alcohol and cigarettes)?*

✳ *Are you cross with someone in particular that you should deal with rather than letting your irritation fly about erratically?*

✳ *Are you sad because something sad has happened: something you may feel you've lost in some way, however small it seems?*

Some people feel almost frightened of happiness when it hits them. They have lived so long tied down painfully by old guilts and anxieties that the new freedom is quite frightening. They wonder what they will do with it. Will they squander it? Will they become horribly selfish? Will their marriage collapse if they feel free and joyful? Does this new feeling mean that they'll become so assertive, so shameless, so self-centred, that no one will ever want to know them?

Well, I can only say, 'Try it and see'. I can say this with confidence, because I know that if you're struggling in the cords of fear or anger or guilt then, when you begin to feel released, you will have a long, long way to go in travelling along the continuum before you reach the other, unattractive pole. Don't refuse to start your journey because of a fear of where it all might end. Instead, enjoy the challenges and pleasures on the way, and realise that you (not others) are in control of just how far you need and want to go.

So remember . . .

You have nothing to lose by recognising and facing up to your negative feelings other than the feelings themselves. Learning to deal with feelings when they come lets you be in control of them, rather than their being in control of you. You can't always stop tough things happening in life, but you can certainly be in charge of how you react to them when they do. Tell yourself each morning, 'Today I give myself permission to feel OK'.

Bibliography

ALBERTI, R. E. *Your perfect right: guide to assertive living*
Impact publications, U.S., 1983.

BECK, A. T. *Love is never enough: overcoming marital misunderstandings through cognitive therapy*
Penguin, 1989.

COOPER, C. L. *The stress check: coping with the stresses of life and work*
Prentice Hall, 1981, o.p.

COZENS, J. *Nervous breakdown: what is it? What causes it? Where to find help*
Piatkus, 1988.

FENSTERHEIM, H. & BAER, J. *Don't say yes when you want to say no*
Futura, 1976.

FRIDAY, N. *My mother/My self.*
Fontana, 1977.

KNIGHT, L. *Talking to a stranger: a consumer's guide to therapy*
Fontana, 1986.

MILLER, A. *The drama of being a child*
Virago, 1987.

MILNER, M. *An experiment in leisure*
Virago, 1986.

NORWOOD, R. *Women who love too much*
Arrow, 1986.

PARKES, C. M. *Bereavement: studies of grief in adult life*
Tavistock, 1986; Penguin, 1986.

PECK, M. S. *The road less travelled*
Century, 1988; Arrow, 1990.

POWELL, K. *Stress in your life*
Thorsons, 1988, o.p.

ROWE, D. *Beyond fear*
Fontana, 1987.

SKYNNER, R. & CLEESE, J. *Families and how to survive them*
Methuen, 1983; pbk, 1984; Mandarin, 1989, o.p.

SOKOLOV, I. & HUTTON, D. *The parents' book: getting on well with our children*
Thorsons, 1988.

WELLS, R. *Helping children cope with grief: facing a death in the family*
Sheldon Press, 1988.

WHOLEY, D. *The courage to change: hope and help for alcoholics and their families: personal conversations with Dennis Wholey*
Fontana, 1986, o.p.

Index